THE STATELESS MARKET

European integration is the most important single issue currently facing the European Union. Underlying most of the disputes between member states is a dilemma that has faced the countries of Western Europe since the end of the last war. Being aware of their weak national positions these states have striven for ever closer cooperation in order to improve their situation. However, by becoming more closely engaged with each other they also fear the erosion of their own national positions.

Paul Kapteyn's book is concerned with this dilemma, whether or not it will be overcome, and what the consequences for Europe and the wider world will be. The process of European integration is unravelled with the help of official documents, articles in newspapers and interviews with business managers, civil servants of the European Commission and of different member states including Belgium, Denmark, France, Germany, the Netherlands and the United Kingdom. Two items in particular get special attention – the Treaty of Schengen on judicial cooperation and harmonization and the problem of EU fraud related to the agricultural subventions. The author also looks in detail at the consequences of the Maastricht Treaty.

Paul Kapteyn places the daily quarrels and conflicts of the EU member states in context and demonstrates that they are part of an ongoing long-term process. This is a book that will enable the student more clearly to understand the complex nature of the debate over European integration and where the results of that process could lead.

Paul Kapteyn is Lecturer in Sociology at the University of Amsterdam.

THE STATELESS MARKET

The European dilemma of integration and civilization

Paul Kapteyn

London and New York

First published as *Markt Zonder Staat* in 1993
by Coutinho BV, the Netherlands

First published in English 1996
by Routledge
11 New Fetter Lane, London EC4P 4EE

Simultaneously published in the USA and Canada
by Routledge
29 West 35th Street, New York, NY 10001

© 1996 Paul Kapteyn

Translated by S.A. Herman

Typeset in Baskerville by
Michael Mepham, Frome, Somerset
Printed and bound in Great Britain by
Mackays of Chatham PLC, Chatham, Kent

British Library Cataloguing in Publication Data
A catalogue record for this book is available from the
British Library

Library of Congress Cataloguing in Publication Data
A catalogue record for this book has been requested

ISBN 0–415–12232–5 (hbk)
ISBN 0–415–12233–3 (pbk)

For Renate

CONTENTS

Preface   viii

1 INTRODUCTION   1

Part I The history

2 THE GOVERNING PRINCIPLES OF MARKET
  AND STATE FORMATION   9

3 THE ORIGINS OF THE EUROPEAN UNION   46

Part II Negotiations

4 THREE SCENARIOS   69

5 THE FIRST EXAMPLE: OPEN BORDERS
  AND THE TREATY OF SCHENGEN   71

6 THE SECOND EXAMPLE: AGRICULTURAL
  POLICY AND AGRICULTURAL FRAUD   92

Part III Conclusions

7 EUROPEAN INTEGRATION   131

8 EUROPEAN CIVILIZATION   158

  Notes   174
  Index   187

PREFACE

'... and the diffident man is, in the end, the more in control.'

(V.S. Naipaul, *New York Review of Books*, Vol. 28, No. 3, 31 January 1991)

This book is about European integration and in particular about the European Union. It provides an overview of the origins of the Union and its subsequent growth. The emphasis is on the acceleration of the integration process that led to the Single European Act of 1986 and in 1992 to the Treaty of Maastricht.

The book also provides more. Far more than the national states themselves, the European Union is a 'developing' organization whose nature and direction form controversial social conflicts. In other words, besides being an established social fact, this international organization is also a social struggle and is discussed here as such.

What made six states decide in 1957 to begin an association they had been incapable of forging before? Why is this integration of states subject to such dramatic changes of pace? How did similar processes develop in the past, and what is so special about today's European integration process? Will this international organization develop into an actual state or will it simply remain a free market? Moreover, what would the consequences be for the national cultures or civilizations, and indeed for 'European civilization' as a whole?

These are questions which this book poses. The answers provide a view of Europe both as a social fact and as a social issue on which the fate of millions hangs, both in and outside the Continent.

The contents of this book are highly diverse. After reviewing earlier market and state-formation processes a model is formed against which the creation of the European Economic Community and its development to the European Union of today is traced. While by its very nature it is a global model, the comparison is rich in details that together highlight the human dimension of social conflict and social cooperation, the corollary of the often anonymous, bureaucratic process.

This book is based on research material from publications, reports and newspaper articles together with many interviews with businessmen, politicians and civil servants from the member states and from the European Union itself whose assistance I gratefully acknowledge.

I have had to search them out in all of Europe's capitals. The European Union does not have a seat in a particular place; it is an association, continually on the move from city to city, where the authority is actually established, the authority of the nation state. I'm glad to be home again.

[12]

1

INTRODUCTION

Opening the Maastricht Treaty, one cannot help but be impressed. Two kings, three queens, one grand duke and six presidents declare their commitment to marking a new step in the process of European integration. They recall the historical importance of ending the division of the European Continent, confirm their attachment to the principles of the rule of law, express the hope for solidarity between peoples and decide in consequence – and for many other reasons – to establish a European Union.[1]

Setting aside this volume and turning to the newspapers, a rather different feeling emerges. The Germans stick to high interest rates while the European Monetary System crumbles about them. The French block the hard-fought trade agreement between the European Union and the United States. Britain and Spain turn against the proposed expansion of the Union because of the perceived reduction in their national influence.

What appears to be happening here? Is this a future European market and state, or is it simply an assembly of states principally concerned with defending their own national interests who wish, moreover, to keep it that way?

This alternating image is typical of the debate between the federalists, who dream of a united Europe, and the nationalists, for whom that ideal is anathema. These groups are neither large nor important. The majority of the people remain undecided and swing between the one vision and the other in a state of personal ambivalence. There is little confidence in any particular outcome and few know precisely what it is that they want.[2]

This uncertainty has never taken dramatic forms. The European integration process, as it unfolded after the Second World War with the formation of the European Economic Community, was the vision of lone idealists together with bureaucrats and related special interest groups such as the agricultural sector, representing highly specific market segments. The broad mass of public opinion expressed little interest. There was no violent negative reaction, but no major support either. In fact it was only in countries that lay somewhat on the periphery, such as Britain and Denmark, that the direction in which these policies were heading became an issue in national politics.

However, this lack of interest soon changed. As the integration process gathered pace in the mid-1980s the population became more well informed and the consequences of integration became less vague. Simultaneously, public discussion became more intense and the ambivalence sharpened. At issue now is the whole question of the economic, political and cultural direction in which this social movement is heading and what this will mean for the more than 300 million people directly involved, and for those indirectly involved distant partners in Central and Eastern Europe as well as in America and the Far East. What is actually happening? Is Western Europe rising from the ashes like a Phoenix, ready to take on the mantle of state as well as market, taking over the tasks once carried out by individual countries? Or is this pure fantasy, like a balloon which, without hot air, has no substance? Put like this, the question has something of the pathos that lifts the discussion above the technical–bureaucratic jargon in which the subject is generally debated.

THE EUROPEAN DILEMMA

The subject of this book is the direction of Europe's integration process and the central dilemma with which the countries of Western Europe have had to deal since the end of the Second World War; the fear of national weakness leads to the need for cooperation, but that same fear prevents them from committing themselves.

Central to this issue is the question of autonomy, which entails the normative expectation that a country's sovereign power cannot be infringed from inside or out. Combining national sovereignty would increase the overall power of the individual countries at the collective level, but the opposite would be true at national level. This dilemma has been a feature of recent history with the launch of a succession of plans after the Second World War designed to paste over the old divisions but which as a result came into conflict with national sovereignty and never transcended the dilemma. The European Economic Community was no exception. Despite becoming the most successful example of European integration with a whole collection of institutions and powers, in principle it nevertheless remained an interstate and intergovernmental institution, one to which the member states delegated powers but not one to which they transferred sovereign powers.

This is understandable. For most of the member states, joining had involved a crucial decision and any formal transfer of sovereignty would have made participation impossible. The low level of integration therefore gave an advantage which was at the same time a disadvantage. The principal aim of the European Community was to form an open internal market for which the member countries would gradually limit their national state controls. Exactly how these controls were to be organized at a Community level remained unclear. With the increasing mutual involvement of state and market interests, if one wanted A then B would not be far behind; the formation of a market would have to entail some form of state. But however obvious this may have seemed, it remained an outsider's view, an opinion that ignored feelings of national pride and identity. In reality, the situation was rather different. A European state would involve transferring sovereignty, which simply went too far for these sentiments of pride and identity.

Those directly concerned were well aware of the lack of proportion between the envisaged market and the intended state controls. However, the problem was brushed over since an open discussion would not bring these state controls any nearer; in fact it might threaten the very formation of a free market. A tacit idea was apparently generally held that the formation of a free market would naturally lead, through the creation of facts, to a concomitant state formation. But that did not happen. Economic integration took shape, albeit slowly and in the face of considerable difficulties, but without the transfer of sovereign powers to a supranational European body. Member states tried to coordinate national controls through intergovernmental negotiations to avoid infringing on national sovereignty, at least directly, while at the same time hoping that a loss of national controls at European level would be compensated.

This was the obvious solution; but because of its intergovernmental character with every country able to exercise a veto the problem remained unsolved. Even though the free market was placed under effective controls in some areas, such as agriculture and exchange rates, further intergovernmental progress proved extremely difficult to achieve. This resulted in the stagnation not only of the development of state controls, but also of the market.

The dilemma intensifies

The tension between market and state intensified and reached a crucial stage with the Single European Act of 1986. Under the terms of this treaty the member states agreed to speed up the liberalization process and to accelerate the free flow of goods, persons, services and capital with a target date of 1992, later postponed to 1993. Yet there was still little public debate about the problem. The focus was on the formation of an open market; the problem of how state controls would be applied to that market was not considered, perhaps even consciously ignored for fear that the resolution might be frustrated again.

However, this situation changed. As the liberalization of the market took shape and state controls began to lag behind, the painful juxtaposition intensified. Limitations to national sovereignty increased without compensation at Community level. Once again the European dilemma raised its ugly head: member countries were prepared to reduce national controls to achieve a free market, but national pride and identity prevented them from transferring national sovereignty.

The discrepancy between the 'negative integration of the market' and the 'positive integration of the state' began to become clear. Because of the refusal to transfer national sovereignty, its limitation was not compensated at supranational level so that what was originally intended as a form of protection became a threat to national culture or civilization. This dilemma applied to all spheres – economic, financial, social, legal and even cultural. Member countries watched as their control over policy was gradually eroded, either by direct prohibitions against national protection or through the introduction of competition for the national industry in the context of a free market, without any proportional compensation at European level. This dilemma also affected national parliaments which, although they may not have formally transferred powers, nevertheless witnessed their democratic rights being diminished as the Single Market took shape, but without an extension of the European Parliament to match.

THE STRUCTURE OF THE BOOK

In the meantime, the Single European Act has taken effect in the context of the European Union, the name by which the Community became known in 1992. The discrepancy between the 'negative integration of the market' and the 'positive integration of the state' are being weighed and measured at various levels. It remains to be seen whether these negotiations will solve the European dilemma. The answer will determine the direction of future European integration and its consequences for national cultures or civilizations.

The discussion is presented as follows: Part I deals with the historical background with Chapter 2 providing a summary of earlier processes of state and market formation from the distant past to the present day. The picture it paints uses historical theory and is partly based on the model developed by sociologist Norbert Elias. Using this model, a wide range of information can be ordered and its regularity shown, described here as the governing principles of the state and market. Like all theories, this model is open to discussion, although that discussion is not pursued here.

The accent in this chapter is on Western Europe, and in particular the history of four countries – France, Britain, Germany and the Netherlands – each of which represent a national variant of a general process of state, market and civilization formation.

In Chapter 3 these insights are then applied to developments since the Second World War in the Transatlantic and European context. Here the focus is on the degree to which the evolution of the European Union corresponds to the regularity previously discussed, and the extent to which it deviates and is therefore unique. European integration is apparently typified by a 'market before state' order – the opposite of all previous processes and in part the reason for its sluggishness. The chapter concludes by asking why there has been a recent acceleration and to what extent the discrepancy between market formation and state formation will be resolved.

Part II is entitled 'Negotiations'. It shows how solutions have been found and applied to the problem of the relationship between state and the market and what the consequences are for national civilizations.

Following a number of possible courses suggested in Chapter 4, these 'scenarios' are then tested in chapters 5 and 6 on the basis of two in-depth studies. The first focuses on the Schengen Agreement and the relaxation of frontier controls. The second focuses more specifically on the European Union, and concerns fraud.

Finally, in Part III recent developments are cited and conclusions drawn in a projection of the most likely course of events for the near future. Chapter 7 is concerned with actual integration, while Chapter 8 discusses the consequences this will have for national civilizations and for European civilization as a whole. Both chapters are more reflective in character and are intended to encourage readers to compare their own opinions about the European integration process with those of the author.

This book is both general in scope and detailed in discussion, but it is written in such a way that readers do not need to be specialists in the subject. For those whose knowledge of world and especially Western European history proves too inadequate, a secondary school history, encyclopedia or some other standard work will certainly provide sufficient basis. For those who wish to find out more about the intellectual background please consult the bibliography and the references in the notes.

Part I
THE HISTORY

2

THE GOVERNING PRINCIPLES OF MARKET AND STATE FORMATION

NO STATES WITHOUT VIOLENCE AND NO FREE MARKETS WITOUT STATES

Two general rules can be derived from earlier state and market formation processes, both characterized by their simplicity. These rules are as follows: 'war is invariably the basis of state formation' and 'free markets evolve within territories of states after they have stabilized'.[1]

Processes of state formation

The principle that state formation is based on violence implies one of two processes. The rule is that one unit of survival expands by conquest and so extends its central functions of violence, taxation and legal monopoly, the triad of controls that typify every state. The exception to the rule is that various survival units may combine to defend themselves against an outside threat. Federal units such as these are generally rather short-lived. They disintegrate as soon as the danger has passed, or are defeated in battle and are compelled to submit their territory to the conqueror.

This rule and its variant are recognizable in all the phases of human state formation. Whether it be the first city states in the misty past, the formation of the great Chinese Empire or later giants such as the United States or the Soviet Union, violent conquest and the fear of violence have consistently provided the motivation for autonomous groups of people to band together and give shape to the central monopolies. These processes start disparately but gradually gain a collective momentum that eventually encompasses all. This is the general direction. Despite the rise of opposing forces and the collapse of larger units, states have grown ever larger, while the scope and complexity of the central administration has invariably increased.

This was how the great state civilizations arose as, over the generations, groups of people of varied origins adapted to one another and to the central controls, which were at first imposed by a small elite on the masses but gradually became linked to the general interest. Central functions would then become increasingly bureaucratic, sometimes even democratic, leading to controls from above and from outside, accepted by those concerned and absorbed as part of the self-control. Increasingly, the state became the focus of identity, the nation, replacing other social units, such as tribe, region or city.

The competition–monopoly mechanism

Developments within states contrasted with that between states. Barely weakened by treaties and mutual promises at an interstate level, the ruling principles have been those of free competition in arms and commerce; while the ever larger states became increasingly 'tame' internally, the level of outward aggression increased. This state of normless rivalry threatens the very existence of states while at the same time providing an explanation for the way they originate and disappear.

This general pattern is neatly captured in the concept of the competition–monopoly mechanism consistently typified in the early city states of Mesopotamia and the banks of the Nile as well as in India and China, and the great empires that subsequently emerged. The process began with the first tribes settling in the deltas of the great rivers of the subtropics where the natural surrounds offered opportunities for a sedentary existence. The new lifestyle proved successful. Food production increased, population grew and a division of labour centred on agriculture and livestock evolved. New groups arrived, attracted by the environment and the success of the first groups.

This process occurred repeatedly, producing successive waves of nomadic tribes descending from Central Asia or perhaps elsewhere and settling on those same fertile soils and learning the new skills. Crucial, and ever more characteristic of this settlement pattern, was that as the process continued, the scarcity of fertile soil increased and the pressure of competition between the various groups grew.

This applied to the settled groups and to outsiders; and as their numbers increased it began to apply between settled groups themselves, with the result that at some stage this latent conflict came out into the open and the parties involved found themselves in a state of war. The struggle was for the most fertile soil and the most strategic positions.

This open and violent competition had disastrous effects for social and physical existence in the short term. Rather different and contrasting effects resulted in the long term. Competition led, as in a tournament, to an imaginary pyramid, with ever more losers and ever fewer winners. Through their success, the winners extended their territory in which they established the triad of control monopolies, first in the form of cities with outlying areas, later in larger regions comprising various integrated centres. At the same time the small and relatively egalitarian tribal units developed into a more stratified or socially tiered state structure headed by a military and a clerical caste. Mutual rivals, these castes held the central functions and controlled the power surplus over the mass of the population which worked the land and produced goods, thereby supplying the surplus of which the select minority disposed.

The history of the ancient Middle Eastern empires reveals this process not to have been entirely continuous; in fact the process occurred in centrifugal and centripetal waves. The momentum of change was slow, so that it seemed to those involved that their state organization was one of absolute values. Nevertheless, central authorities continually found themselves facing overwhelming problems of internal control and external attack and finally succumbing to this double threat, either collapsing or falling prey to a new and larger conglomerate.

Part of this movement was formed by the Jewish people, whose history is told in the Old Testament from a religious 'us' perspective and as such has become world-renowned.[2] Unintentionally perhaps, the Old Testament also offers a valuable insight into early state formation processes. The nomadic tribes were attracted by the fertile banks of the River Jordan and managed to conquer an area from the tribes already settled there. Later, the struggle continued both internally and externally until, after a period of more or less successful encounters described in the Book of Judges, three successive kings – Saul, David and Solomon – managed to establish the central monopolies in a particular territory and to introduce a certain stability. It was not long, however, before the tide turned and

11

the state split, falling to the conqueror and finally being absorbed into a larger unit.

It was a fate that many states met, as the struggle to preserve their independence suddenly switched from essential to useless. Often, even the memory of the struggle was erased with the loss of autonomy. Occasionally, the story was preserved, like a seed that keeps its nucleus for centuries. But whenever an opportunity arose for a lost state to revive its fortunes, it invariably succeeded through war.

Europe

In Europe the competition–monopoly mechanism was also the driving force behind state formation. With the disintegration of the Roman Empire, which succumbed under the double burden of internal control problems and external threat, nomadic tribes from Central Asia once again descended on Europe. They chased the tribes ahead of them on and into the exposed Roman provinces, carving out territories amid the ruins of this state-based civilization at the expense of the tribes who were already living there.

After this period of mass migration a new integration process began, of which the centre was Western Europe. Despite opposition from many quarters, this development was to provide a continuity that extends to today's state formation processes in Europe and the world at large, and of which the recent European integration process is just a part.

The formation of the Frankish kingdom in the seventh and eighth centuries revealed the first tendency towards integration. The central figure was Charlemagne, who managed to assemble major areas of the Western Roman Empire under his rule. This first Western European empire did not last long. After the death of Charlemagne, his kingdom began to fall apart and, furthermore, after his son's death the disintegration assumed an official form with the Treaty of Verdun in 843; the more Latin oriented part in the west and the Germanic part in the east were separated by the middle kingdom of Lotharingia. This situation came about because there were three sons, but in fact the middle kingdom hardly existed as an independent unit.

This division of the Frankish empire marked the start of the centrifugal and centripetal movements, dominated by the problem of internal controls and external threats. The connection is obvious. The more successful a monarch was in conflicts and the greater the monarch's territory, the more power had to be delegated to local authorities able to exercise royal power by proxy. This led to the crucial question of how to keep these local representatives under control and prevent them from carving out their own power base. This problem was resolved by appointing trusted individuals who had proved their worth in battle and who received conquered land in lien as a reward. However, this widely used system of feudalized early state controls provided no guarantee. Success on the battlefield repeatedly proved to be a double-edged sword; vassals naturally drew away from the authority of their liege-lord, even if the royal court was itinerant with its watchful eye in every corner of the country. If the barons were successful in resisting royal power, often with aid from elsewhere, the domain disintegrated and the vassal was able to act as the sovereign – only to be faced with the same problem of how to safeguard a growing territory.

These opposing movements first came to an end in countries with comparatively clear natural frontiers. External threats were less prominent in countries surrounded by the sea or by mountains, while considerable difficulties stood in the way of increasing integration in countries where no strong frontiers formed a natural defence. This difference in the level of 'integration threshold' can be seen in the relatively early integration of the French and English territories compared with the later, rather more problematic integration of the German and Slav areas.

This geographically determined integration threshold also explains why the European integration process failed to lead to a stable, state system covering the whole or most of the Continent. After Charlemagne, later attempts to attain this occurred within the context of the French integration process during the Napoleonic era and that of the German integration process during the Second World War. Both failed, the reason being that Europe is divided by the Pyrennean, Alpine and Carpathian mountain ranges into regions that are easy to defend and hard to conquer. More important for forces moving east has been the lack of any high barriers from which to defend conquered territory. As a result, the continuous struggle on the eastern front has repeatedly weakened the relatively easily defended western front; Europe remains vulnerable to attack from two sides. Both Napoleon and Hitler fought wars on two fronts, neither of which were mistakes as much as they proved to be strategic necessities which were unavoidable and fatal.

Because of its geography, Europe as a whole therefore has a high integration threshold which has also influenced the problems of interstate relations in Eastern Europe. They owed their survival to the endlessness of the space around them, which made it impossible for the countries of the West to permanently annex the East while at the same time making their own integration difficult. Centrifugal and centripetal forces alternated; indeed, the strongly repressive integration under Russian tsarist and communist rule and the present disintegration show that this pattern of alternation has lost none of its force.

The high European integration threshold does not imply that violent integration may not happen at some time in the future and that a European state can never be formed. It explains the lack of such an organization up to the present day and the familiar division into West, Central and Eastern Europe reflected in constitutional terms as well as in terms of economic markets and civilizations.

The problem of the European integration threshold illustrates the central point at issue here. Violence has always been the basis of state formation, so that geographical details have influenced events through their strategic value.

Market formation processes

Just as the myth of a natural, biologically based affinity is connected to a state, the market is associated with the fictitious ideal of a natural, unfettered trade that once existed, fell into disuse and is now due for repair. It is true that people have bartered since ancient times, or at least since they started producing more than they actually needed. But these markets were not 'free'. As old as the markets themselves are the controls imposed 'from above' in the form of taxation in kind or in money, but also in the form of protection against external violence and competition and as a guarantee of the internal relations. The connection between the command relations of the state and the exchange relations of the market is clear. Trade depends on the certainty that a satisfactory barter is honoured, that there is some sort of central authority to ensure that the system of barter does not become robbery and that some form of legal and material infrastructure exists through which to make and enforce agreements. This control depends on a reciprocal arrangement; taxation is essential to support this system. Although taxpayers always complain that taxes are too heavy and are unfairly levied, the principle of taxation is not questioned.

The state serves the market, but the market also serves the state. Central authority benefits from a prosperous trade and the concomitant productivity; after all, this is the state's income and it offers the opportunity, in addition to market formation, of representing interests which are not perhaps directly linked to the economy. An example is the honour or status of the ruling elite and the associated military and legal organizations. A contrasting example is formed by the fate of the less prosperous members of society. As peripheral as they may be, they belong to the same unit of state and market as the elite and because they are the object of concern their need for care has to be met.

These relationships can also be identified at an early stage. Among the small nomadic units trade remained limited, as did the internal and external labour and production differential. The borderline between barter and robbery was always subtle. With the formation of larger sedentary units, conditions changed. Within a unit of authority, part of the total production was demanded by force in the form of taxation, while internal exchange became less risky and therefore more profitable. Under this protection, the market grew from local barter to a network that in theory covered the territory of the state and in which the advantages of the differential led to greater wealth. This applied principally to the elite, but also to the merchants and producers who formed the market, and finally to the peasants and artisans who conducted the actual work. The territorial nature of trade, i.e. the unity of state and market, was reflected in the mutual interests of military, religious, commercial and artisan groups. Success in conflict would depend on the amount of taxation levied, which in turn depended on the productivity of the country. At the same time, this productivity benefited from the military and legal protection of the state. The unity of state and market was also apparent from the limitations on external trade. This cross-frontier commerce is a particularly intriguing element, but it was actually quite limited. Finally, the unity is shown in what is described as the downfall of these empires. This process is also subject to a vicious circle – one that is weakening rather than strengthening. Thus the problems connected with controls fragmented the protected market, leading first to reduced production and then to falling tax revenues. As a result, the means to exercise controls were in turn reduced, so that the problems of control increased even more.

Europe

A similar picture is seen in relations between state and market in European development, although these are more complex and require a more detailed description.

The complexity is a result of Europe's so-called 'political fragmentation', which is itself the result of geographical fact. According to the theory employed here, which couples the growth and decline of markets and states, the economic development of this continent should actually be lagging behind that of countries such as China, with its long-standing political unity. Europe in fact did lag behind, until a sustained acceleration in European economic development began in the late Middle Ages. This European acceleration is intriguing because economic growth was not accompanied by an acceleration in the political sphere. In fact, instead of the expected parallel between the formation of market and state the opposite appears to have been the case.[3]

To understand how this worked, the period from the fourteenth to the nineteenth century should be divided into two. In the first phase, running from approximately 1300 to 1600, trade became concentrated in a number of cities in northern Europe which, in the shape of the Hanseatic League, were able to take various measures to provide greater freedom and protection while never actually creating an overall central authority. At the same time, the famous cities of Central and Northern Italy flourished, forming an even more divided political group whose members regularly fought each other in various combinations. Nevertheless, this was the economic hub of Europe. In the sixteenth century, however, the focus moved to the cities of Holland whose autonomy was subject to remarkably few limitations within a confederate structure. This Dutch Republic emerged from a successful resistance to the House of Habsburg's attempts to strengthen its authority over the Netherlands by centralizing taxation. Economic growth was in parallel with political fragmentation in these three regions, with the possible result that taxes were kept low through a relaxed central authority and much of the profits could then go directly into new investment.

This connection is probably correct. In Europe, the result was that the commercial classes found themselves generally opposed to the old military, aristocratic elites, and central authority. They eventually gained a position that was stronger than similar groups elsewhere. The differences are clear. While in other parts of the world unity of command continued to dominate trade, in Europe the central control functions came to be dominated more by the subjects themselves through their democratic representatives than by the sovereign.

It is tempting to conclude from this link between political fragmentation and economic growth that from the end of the Middle Ages, market formation gained the lead over state formation and eventually brought about a capitalist world market to which states have been forced to conform. However, that is not quite correct. However prosperous the city states and leagues were, in the end their lack of central protection led to their downfall.

This pattern first developed inland. Political fragmentation had kept taxation relatively low, particularly in the regions already discussed. However, this also resulted in a large number of customs duties on trade between and within the state alliances with their weak central authority. The merchants themselves saw these duties as impediments to trade, forcing them to find other ways of conducting business. Moreover, another result of this fragmentation was the increasing risk to merchandise – this became a particular bone of contention.[4]

Because of these conditions, trade tended to expand more at sea than on land during this period so that cities with good maritime connections found themselves strategically placed. And yet the same problems were to emerge at sea as on land, although perhaps in a less striking fashion. Tolls on the principal sea routes caused considerable irritation which regularly led to armed resistance. The argument ran that the sea should be free for all; in fact it was more of a free-for-all as the ships of the time show, with shipwrights being forced to compromise between merchantmen and men-of-war and trading vessels often resembling pirate ships. As we have seen, this political fragmentation produced the economic advantage of low taxation, but the emphasis gradually switched to the disadvantages of low security and the multitude of customs duties, both of which constricted the market's growth.

This change occurred because elsewhere in Europe the state's functions were expanding and had begun to delineate a market within an established state territory. These markets were able to develop an unparalleled internal freedom because of the protection of the state.

It was in Britain and France that national free internal markets developed within which regional tolls were lifted and converted into one central tax together with import and export duties at the state's frontiers. This further strengthened the link between state and market. Their mutual interdependence gave them an advantage in the military and commercial competition between states, at first against Europe's old city states and leagues in Germany, Italy and Holland which had failed to keep pace in state formation, and later globally in competition with state systems on other continents. This development occurred during the second phase between approximately 1600 and 1900, in which an initial period of mercantilist national protectionism saw the formation of national internal markets followed by a subsequent moderate liberalization of interstate trade. Even so, despite the attraction of a 'global market' and the undoubted increase in prosperity as a result, the domestic market remained the main area of economic activity. For the eighteenth-century Scottish customs official and ethical philosopher Adam Smith, it formed 'perhaps one of the principal causes' of the prosperity enjoyed by Great Britain and other large countries. As we have seen, it was not formed before the state had established its authority over a specific territory; indeed, it specifically followed the stabilization of the central means of coercion.[5]

The strong ties between state and market were again revealed in the early twentieth century when the nineteenth-century liberalization made way for renewed protectionism of national markets. The result was economic and military disaster, but it ultimately led to the formation of larger units, among them today's European Union. The question is whether the historical pattern we have noted here is established or contradicted by this latest development.

NATIONAL VARIANTS IN THE FORMATION OF STATE, MARKET AND CIVILIZATION

Before discussing more recent developments in Europe, the two imperatives of state and market formation will be examined in the light of developments of various separate units which now form part of the European Union. These national variations in exchange and authority relations govern the differences between national civilizations and, as will become apparent below, are felt all the more intensely as the contemporary integration process progresses.

Similarities

In a comparison with societies in other parts of the world, it is the similarities that are particularly striking. The four countries discussed here – France, Britain, the Netherlands and Germany – have enjoyed a long history as social units in which the functions of the state have been extended to cover ever-increasing aspects of life. This is true of the repressive functions of the police, justice and taxation, whose scope has widened but whose repressive activities have been reduced. The same applies to the so-called 'soft-sector' functions such as education, health and housing.

Markets grew in direct relation to this development. Their functions were increasingly split and linked at a higher level, which meant that productivity rose across the board and national wealth grew. As a result there was an increase in the level of mutual dependence and vulnerability. On the one hand, there was a concentration of the opportunities for power and control and on the other hand, there was a reduction of the internal differences between the various population groups. Directly connected with this was that the basic circumstances of life became less the responsibility of the family, class organization, or the city or region with their authoritarian and hierarchic relations and their tendency towards group pressure. State organizations gradually took over custodianship of the nation's welfare, relations were increasingly collectivized and levelled while at the same time individual freedom of action increased.

This movement occurred on all fronts. Whether it was rulers and ruled, masters and apprentices, men and women or parents and children, all those involved found themselves having to deal with one another increasingly as equals and in that sense to pay more attention to their own actions. The mutual control that people exercised over each other became more equal, or rather less unequal, more stable or steady and so less immediately emotional, while its scope increased. In this way this external control generated a self-control with similar characteristics. People's fear of random violence from their superiors and inferiors diminished, thus giving them greater freedom. This freedom was in its turn, however, limited by a fear of failing to meet the expectations of egalitarianism and becoming too authoritarian or obedient. These pangs of conscience grew so that the level of national identification – or in a wider sense, of national civilization – rose, while the fears attached to the more small-scale authoritarian relations diminished.

As with the formation of market and state, this process took place over many centuries, with periods of interspersed stagnation and acceleration. Recent decades have in particular seen increased consideration by citizens for each others' interests at national level, a development noticeable also in complaints about the lack of consideration. To a considerable extent this 'acquisition' is protected by state arrangements, so that the question concerns what is or will be the connection between national civilizations on the one hand and the European integration process on the other.[6]

National variants

In this case, a useful area in which to measure national similarities and differences is customs policy. This state-operated organization controls the cross-frontier traffic of goods and the duties to which this traffic is subject. It therefore serves the interests of the state and the free internal market, just as the police do in various ways by controlling the flow of persons. The two organizations are also comparable in their military mould; for example, in their strict ranking, in the division between lower and higher ranks, in the wearing of uniforms, in their own training system and in some countries the carrying of arms. Moreover, the *esprit de corps* is characterized by a definite hierarchic solidarity, not only within the organization but also towards the country as a whole, personified in state authority.

In short, the customs service is one of the pillars of an established society, and as with the police, the reason for this is the essential function it carries out. The one serves the age-old state monopoly on the use of violence and the other on taxation. The development of both organizations is inextricably linked to that of the state.

This is probably most evident in the case of the police,[7] whose task, that of keeping order, was previously fulfilled by military force. This changing of the guard took place a considerable time after a central authority had been established and external threats had been removed. This span of time between external and internal pacification by the central authority did not imply that the use of civil force went unchecked within the borders of the new territory. At that time public order was maintained to a greater or lesser degree not by the state but by the local authorities on the basis of their previous autonomy, the military aspect of which they had been forced to relinquish. These are clearly two distinct phases. The conquest of foreign territory is a more dangerous, but at the same time a simpler task than permanent pacification. Besides the logistic problems involved in setting up a central apparatus, emotional problems also play a role. The order is no longer 'Attack!' but 'Prevent others from attacking!' and this preventive role requires more empathy, forethought and restraint on the part of the system as a whole and each individual within it. Such an organization cannot simply be forced onto a population, but demands a certain measure of endorsement, which is gained by not snubbing the existing authorities, at least not in the short term and not under the prevailing conditions.

These relationships changed. Even though certain police functions continued to be organized on a local or regional basis, the central authority increased its control and gradually, with various differences in tempo and degree, a national police force was created. The formation of what was increasingly a bureaucratic and professional organization was unmistakably in the interests of the central rather than the local authorities. The overwhelming majority were ambivalent towards this. At first, people experienced the new authority as another form of repression, but as the market and state networks became broader and denser on a national level, maintaining public order on the same level came to be increasingly in the interests of the citizens. Their criticism was therefore levelled not at the police and judicial systems as such, but at their influence over them, which, it was felt, needed to be increased. They managed to get their way to some degree as central authorities became more democratic as well as bureaucratic. This did not take place directly but through representation in national parliaments, which in their turn formed part of an increasing centralization and the merging of state and citizens' interests.

The development of the police mirrored that of the customs service.[8] The formation of this organization took place long after the state had stabilized its authority on a military basis. This is an illustration of the proposition that the order of events is 'market after state'. As in the case of the police, the difference between these phases does not imply that there had previously been no restrictions. On the contrary, the erection of national economic boundaries did not mean state control of a market which had previously been free, but a liberation of the market, at least within the national boundaries, from the many local levies. As we have seen, the formation of a free market takes place after the authority of the state has already been stabilized to some extent. In this case too, the establishment of a central regulatory body such as the customs department served not only the interests of state control, but also that of traders and business people. The losers were once again the traditional nobility, who after relinquishing their military autonomy still functioned in the areas of policing and taxation for a considerable period, sometimes on their own authority, but more often as a kind of delegated tax collecting service, handing over a fixed amount to the central authorities and keeping the remainder for themselves. The problems for the state and the population inherent in this system were evident, but they could only be remedied after the economic networks had reached a level at which commercial and political interests converged nationally and dominated those of the local authorities.

France – hierarchical centralism

Of the four countries under discussion here, France demonstrates most clearly the relationship described above. The process of state formation in France is modelled almost entirely on the competition–monopoly mechanism. In a long series of violent upheavals, which began after the break-up of the Frankish empire in the ninth century, a national unity was formed with Paris at its centre. Most of the new possessions were claimed in the fifteenth century when the English Normans were defeated in the west and the Burgundians in the east. In the seventeenth and eighteenth centuries, especially in the east and north, more territory was gained, and with this the present borders of France were established with a few exceptions. The balance of power in France reflects this linear development. State authority was established centrally and even today the machinery of government is characterized by a strongly centralized and hierarchic structure, which is accorded the highest status once reserved for the sovereign and which fills its subjects on the one hand with national pride and on the other with suspicion. The nation state has undoubtedly become an important symbol of identification, but the ties felt towards it are as ambivalent as the regime is authoritarian. In this kind of system, people obey for the most part because they must or because it suits them; but given the choice, they prefer not to.

Economic relationships can be seen in a similar light. In France, the government is less a third party standing aloof from the market than in other countries. It participates through its own companies and in this way directly influences market and labour relations. It does not, as is often the case elsewhere, determine the limits within which employers and employees can negotiate, but by negotiating itself, as the strongest party, it influences the outcome.[9] French society thus has the characteristics of a command economy, in which negotiation or solidarity, as a means of enabling cooperation between parties, are less important than orders from above.

The origins of these relationships have their roots far back in history. Charlemagne governed his empire from several residences and was continually travelling between them in order to preserve unity through his personal presence and military followers. This peripatetic rule remained an important form of central control in later forms of state. Even though under the feudal system of that time, the sovereign delegated his governing authority to trusted retainers, the master's eye remained, even in these relationships, a necessary means of maintaining central authority and limiting his representatives' freedom of manoeuvre. The effect, however, was limited, resulting in an alternation of integrating and disintegrating movements.

This period of shifting trends came to an end, in addition to the geographical boundaries of French territory mentioned earlier, as a result of the increasing monetarization of market transactions and social relationships in general. The connection is clear; in an economy based on simple barter even the sovereign was forced to pay in kind for services and this meant that the area in which his army was stationed would become subject to tax. The sovereign would give part of the conquered territory to the army commander in lien.

There were serious disadvantages to this system. The inhabitants soon became disgruntled and there was a good chance that vassals might start up for themselves. But what was the alternative? The vicious circle was broken with the growth of trade and the increasing role of money as the medium of exchange. This economic growth and the monetarization of trade was conditioned by the political fragmentation of this period. The effects, however, were different. Above a certain level, the sovereign no longer had to levy taxes in kind, instead he received money with which he paid for services. This meant that an important centrifugal force of the feudal system disappeared and the system as a whole was greatly weakened.

Moreover the sovereign gained more direct power because the use of money demanded a form of central guarantee and not surprisingly he was the one to provide it.

The link between growing monetarization and centralization became increasingly apparent during the course of the Middle Ages. The connection became even stronger in the following period when, in the fifteenth century, the borders of the state and the accompanying monopoly of force by the military had stabilized, and as an extension of this the tax monopoly had increased its functions.[10] The classic example is the introduction of the first general direct taxation. This was the *taille*, a tax which vassals had previously owed to their liege-lord, or rather one which they collected for him, and which was now levied directly from the centre on every subject with property. This undermined the position of the local authorities, even though this encroachment was softened and concealed by the nobility's exemption from it. The scope of this new tax was thus limited and the central sovereign remained heavily dependent on the local nobility. It is significant that the successful sixteenth-century sovereign Francis I – a century after the *taille* had been introduced – still felt compelled to maintain an itinerant court, just as Charlemagne had centuries earlier.

The slow but steady strengthening of the central monopolies manifested itself not only in a property tax but also in the introduction of a tax on trade. This demonstrated how difficult it was, in spite of the fact that the central authority had already been stabilized, to organize a free internal market whose borders were guaranteed by a national customs service. Trade was not free, but traditionally subjected to all kinds of tolls levied by local authorities, part of which the central authority tried with more or less success to procure. This state of affairs united the state and traders. Both tried to replace the various levies with a central uniform tax which, if collected at the national borders would not only fill the national treasury but also free the internal market. In addition, the central tax also protected the market from foreign competition through high import duties, sometimes accompanied by export subsidies, which according to the notions of the time would be paid for from abroad. The theory of mercantilism is often seen as legitimizing the ambitions of the centralizing state but it was intended to be of equal service to the merchant class, as became apparent in 1614 when the French States General submitted a first request to form a free internal market.[11] The position of the central authority was not yet strong enough in that period to carry out this unification at the expense of the local authorities. This was to take place fifty years later in the reign of Louis XIV, at least a century after Francis I. In this way the minister responsible, Jean-Baptiste Colbert, the son of a merchant, served both the interests of his king and his own roots. In addition, part of his plan was an initiative to establish state-run businesses, by which he showed just how closely state and market were linked. As mentioned earlier, this position of the state is typically French. This was especially true for mercantilism, which was in line with the developing centralist–hierarchical structure of the state.

This structure appears, at first sight, to be all the more firmly established because there was a strong and effective compulsion to obey. However, that is a misunderstanding which fails to take account of the relative nature of power. The French state machinery became so authoritarian exactly because the centrifugal counter-forces were equally strong, although not strong enough to permanently frustrate the integration of the state. Certainly the nobility as the defeated local authorities of the past adapted themselves to the new state of affairs reluctantly and incompletely. They remained a separate class outside the system, considering work beneath their dignity and refusing to commit themselves to the bourgeois market. One of the results of this disdain, the result of an inability to accept their loss of status, was that the market in France had to function without the former elite, which meant that the scale of agrarian production in particular remained small. This led to the introduction of initiatives by the central authority. In consequence, the state seemed ambitious and dominant, as indeed it was, but this tendency should be seen in relation to the opposing tendencies, and then the net result seems more modest. This deceptive exterior is still apparent in what we have seen, for example, of how people identify with the national state. On the one hand the state demands respect but on the other it is regarded with suspicion.

This was even more true in the seventeenth century when the initiative for a free internal market was introduced. Colbert's plans came after the central authority had to some extent already been established, but they were too early to guarantee success. On paper the first concession was made by limiting the integration to twelve northern provinces, but even that proved too much. Not all internal levies were actually abandoned and, after some time, old levies which had disappeared began to reappear.

Moreover, the operation of the new system remained in the

hands of local tax-collectors instead of a bureaucratic professional customs organization. In this way uniformity was splintered by particularist interests. For at least a century, France had to make do with these discordant relationships, until the central authority began to enforce the system consistently. This was shortly after the French Revolution. Only then was the central authority strong enough – and the opposition of the aristocracy sufficiently weakened – to produce a free internal market that was professionally protected and guarded. Certainly in the beginning, during the notorious French Continental System, this double function was carried out in a strongly repressive military fashion. However, it would be wrong to view this period as an exception. French economic policy was, both before and after that time, strongly protectionist, which earned the operators, the customs department, the reputation of being aggressive, authoritarian and inconsistent. It was reflected in the weapons which the officers carried, as well as the way in which they were rewarded. This consisted of a share of the 'spoils', which thus resembled the despised tax-collecting system of the past. Characteristically, French customs officials did not differentiate between genuine mistakes and intentional deception, except when it suited them.

This anti-trade image was softened, as actual practice was in the following years, but the same ingredients remained. In fact, French customs officials still carry weapons, their pay still consists of a premium related to the 'spoils', and 'intent' still has no official part in determining the level of punishment.[12]

Britain – egalitarian centralism

The formation of the British state shows clear similarities with the situation in France. Here too, a violent competitive struggle between smaller units led eventually to the formation of a large-scale organization, which presaged a long, historical continuity in England and which gained a large measure of acceptance. The last battle to be waged by the central authority on the island (in reality, merely a skirmish) was in the mid-eighteenth century, when Scotland, already bound to England in many ways, formally became a part of the kingdom. As in France, the British state forms an important symbol of identity. However, the machinery of the state is built less along hierarchic–centralist lines and its outer display is more modest. This means that the ties between the population and the state are less ambivalent. Central controls are less authoritarian and rely more on negotiation and mutual respect, while the population for its part mistrusts the state's authority less and avoids obedience to the regime less than in France.[13]

These characteristics of the relationship between state and individual have a long history. They are related to differences in the formation of the state, which in turn depend on geographical differences. Britain is an island kingdom and as such is surrounded by a natural border, the sea. France also has a nautical boundary in the south and west and there are mountains in the east and south. But there are no such barriers in the north. The terrain merges imperceptibly with the Low Countries, today's Belgium and the Netherlands. Further to the east, beyond the hills of the Ardennes to those of the Vogeze, lies the open countryside of Alsace-Lorraine, bordered by the Rhine. But this river does not pose a serious obstacle for anyone wishing to cross it, nor does the land beyond. This accessibility made France vulnerable and led to a long series of competitive struggles between the French and Habsburg sovereigns, who both coveted these areas in the east and north for their wealth and access to the sea. Moreover, neither wanted to relinquish this important defensive area to the other. This struggle lasted well into the seventeenth and eighteenth centuries with France eventually gaining the upper hand and able, at least for the time being, to claim victory. An important condition for success was that France managed to cover its back and, unlike its main rival, did not have to fight on two fronts. This advantage did not preclude the necessity for the central authority to exert itself to the utmost and organize the state in the interests of the struggle. The result was a strongly hierarchic–centralist state structured more or less along military lines, exactly because there was such a great risk of a centrifugal movement.

This is where England and France differed. The English process of state formation was the direct result of an invasion by the Duke of Normandy, which made him a worthy rival of the French sovereign of whom he was a vassal. Their struggle led eventually to the French king's victory, with the result that the Normans retreated to their island where they established a feudal structure replacing the previous Saxon one. The French vassal was now the English liege-lord and his French retainers the new English vassals. Thus the French-speaking aristocracy positioned themselves above the previous Germanic-speaking noble elite, after which both people and language blended into a new entity.

There were other differences between the developments in the English and French territories. While the French state apparatus became centralized under pressure from the continuing wars, which meant the central authority strengthened its position at the expense particularly of the local nobility, in England the increase in power at the centre remained limited, as did the loss of power on the part of the English nobility. The reason for this is obvious. English territory was more difficult to attack and easier to defend, so there was less need of a strongly centralized hierarchic authority.

A well-known example of the relatively strong position of the nobility is the famous Magna Carta of 1215. This strong position can also be seen from other formalized rights and duties which compelled the sovereign to ask permission for each tax separately, while the French *taille*, although a later innovation, was introduced without any consultation of parliament. The French king was thus above the law while the English monarch was subject to it. This difference in status was also reflected in external display. The English court had little of the grandeur of the French. It was simply less of a court, less the centre of state affairs and intrigues, less the top of a status pyramid in which hierarchic command relationships were distilled, and also less the focus of cultural refinement. The English sovereigns remained, even in the sixteenth and seventeenth centuries, when their position grew stronger, more a first among equals. They focused both as rulers and for their pleasure on the aristocracy who were still situated rurally, while in France it was the aristocracy who, whether they liked it or not, were forced to focus on the court of the sovereign.

Britain's natural borders and the effect that these had on the nation's development led quickly to the accepted notion that its government was less centralized than that of France. Britain traditionally, the argument continues, has a comparatively unassertive and restrained central government and, partly because of this, a comparatively free market, which especially from the nineteenth century onwards was a model for the rest of the world and which in a certain sense expanded to become the world market. But this is not actually the case.[14] Britain as a kind of natural example of the free market is a fiction which arose when the British market freed itself from earlier restrictions and aligned itself with the dominant ideology of the nineteenth century – liberalism.

The facts present a different story. The most striking difference with France is not that the comparative safety of Britain led to a lesser degree of centralization; it is that the geographical advantage resulted in less of a barrier to integration, so that the centralization process developed more easily and for this reason took hold earlier and subsequently became less hierarchical and absolutist and more egalitarian and democratic.

Important elements in this development were the Magna Carta and the emergence of parliament – the House of Lords followed by the House of Commons. These typically British constructions point to the limited power of the sovereign compared to France and coupled with this was the relatively important power of the local nobility. But there is an even more important difference. These institutions, unlike the weaker French States General, were not primarily there to represent local interests against the central authority. On the contrary, they formed part of this authority primarily as a way of maintaining control. In other words, a negotiation relationship arose in which the sovereign and the nobility together, in spite of their mutual differences, comprised the central authority, while in France a command system emerged in which the king made the decisions.

Many examples of this early form of democratic or egalitarian centralism can be found, some of which were mentioned by the French writer de Toqueville at the beginning of the nineteenth century, such as the uniformity of law, the currency and the property taxes. Not only were these forms of democratic centralism introduced earlier in Britain than in France, they also contained fewer exemptions and did not spare the aristocracy. Last in this list come the uniformity, centralization and 'externalization' of the taxes on trade, which were introduced in Britain earlier than in France, but similarly only after the establishment of the central state authority during the course of the thirteenth century and which limited at an early stage the many different locally levied tolls.[15]

Another difference was the commercial interest of the aristocracy. The English barons accepted the loss of their previous military status much earlier than their French counterparts, and sublimated this loss in hunting and other forms of 'sport'. This gave them the opportunity to concentrate on the commercial exploitation of their land. The result was that the contrast between the aristocratic upper class and the middle-class small farmers, businessmen and traders became relatively small in Britain. It is interesting to note that, as if to demonstrate this relationship, the English language has no word of its own for 'bourgeois'. Clearly, this general market orientation contributed to the early commercialization of relations in Britain and thus to the growth of the internal market. This was the basis of the fast growth of British prosperity, especially in the eighteenth century, and its later colonial expansion.

The fact that there was an early and relatively egalitarian centralism does not imply that the English state apparatus already possessed an effective civil service and parliamentary control. Developments in this direction took longer. Here also, there was considerable tension between the sovereign, the aristocracy and the middle classes. As in France, the crown was able to strengthen its position during the sixteenth and seventeenth centuries through foreign competition with the Dutch Republic – and also with France and Spain – and the resultant policy of protectionist mercantilism with the notorious Navigation Acts. In Britain, however, these absolutist ambitions were counteracted by more egalitarian relations. In the mid-seventeenth century Charles I overestimated his chances. He was deposed and beheaded. After a tumultuous period of changing coalitions the monarchy was restored, after which the development towards egalitarian–centralism accelerated. Thus the English revolutions, like the French Revolution a century later, provided favourable conditions for the further development of the internal market. Towards the end of the seventeenth century and at the beginning of the eighteenth, the English Customs and Excise was set up in its modern form. This meant further bureaucratization and professionalization, in which the lease system was replaced by a fixed salary with a pension. This was intended to increase the reliability of the service and was unique for its time.

English customs officers did not carry weapons as in France. This had little to do with the difference in the level of the tariffs (they were not so different in this period) but with the comparatively high level of pacification which English society had reached.

In the nineteenth century the difference in economic policy between the two countries increased. Both lowered their tariffs, but Britain went much further than France, with the mutual balance of power becoming the determining factor. In 1700 this favoured France which was geographically and demographically the larger, but a century later Britain had the upper hand.

British military and commercial dominance was established and strengthened after the Napoleonic period. Based on a strong internal market and a strong navy as a means of attack and defence, the British state and market expanded to new continents. The accompanying ideology was no longer mercantilist but liberal, and this was possible because, in contrast with the period of more defensive mercantilism, Britain's own position was so strong that many an 'honest' competitive struggle would be won on a military and economic basis. France and other countries followed the liberal path, partly as a result of British dominance. The world market did not become 'free', as did the principal internal markets. Most countries were not sufficiently convinced of their own strength and Britain, however strong it was, lacked the authority to demand this. In the second half of the nineteenth century, with the arrival of a united Germany on the world stage, international competitive pressure increased and British supremacy began to wane. As a result the liberal belief in a free market without a state lost its persuasiveness in favour of a new mercantilist protectionism. Nevertheless it was Britain which maintained the free trade doctrine, of which it had been the most important protector and profiteer, until the Great Depression of the 1930s when, as the last of the major powers, it joined the spiral of national protectionism.

In view of this rise and fall of liberal ideology, it would have seemed obvious for the control exerted by the British customs to have remained less strict and authoritarian than in France and even to have decreased in strength. More so than in France, Britain was not only a producer but also a trader in domestic and foreign products, with London being the hub of this world market. Yet when the protection was for health rather than purely economic reasons, British customs could be strict and inflexible. This defensive attitude more generally typified the bourgeois–aristocratic gentlemen, who because of the international dominance of their island kingdom felt superior to the rest of the world. As often happens, when this position came under threat and the fear of losing this status grew, so also did the perceived need to maintain a 'distance', turning into a compulsive fear of contamination by foreigners which was legitimized on medical grounds. This mixture of insecurity about status and economic liberalism still characterizes the 'control culture' of British customs and more generally British dealings with other countries. On the one hand this is strongly nationalist and on the other it is cosmopolitan. Internal dealings take place on a more egalitarian basis than in France, directed less towards command and obedience and more towards negotiation and mutual respect. This description is relative however, and does not deny the existence of traditional class differences, which still determine social customs. Of more recent interest, the egalitarian advantage which Britain enjoyed over France and other European countries seems to have diminished, most importantly because of the differences in economic growth and social levelling.

The Netherlands – egalitarian federalism

The Dutch process of state formation followed a different course than in France and Britain, the crucial difference being that national unity was achieved through a reaction towards a common external enemy rather than through actual conquest. The form that the state took in the marshy delta of the Rhine, Meuse and IJssel, protected from the sea by a line of dunes, was established as a federal construction, in which the common people rather than the nobility played the leading role. Consequently, there was little pressure to move towards centralism and the relationships between and within the provinces were comparatively egalitarian. After approximately two centuries, this federal construction came to an end when a centralist structure was imposed on the country during the Napoleonic period. This structure was retained after sovereignty was regained at the beginning of the nineteenth century. Thus the Dutch state changed from a 'burgher' republic into a citizen's monarchy, which then further developed in the direction of egalitarian–centralism.

The Republic of the United Provinces was founded in the midsixteenth century when several Dutch cities and provinces combined into a defensive alliance, the Union of Utrecht, in a more or less common struggle. They were fighting against the Spanish House of Habsburg which, in the person of Philip II, maintained central control over both the northern and southern Netherlands with Brussels as its capital. The immediate cause of this resistance was the monarch's efforts to increase central authority, whereby the taxation system would be centralized and unified. This sort of initiative had been taken earlier by Charles V, Philip II's father, who had introduced a new system of criminal law throughout the Low Countries and had managed to create something of a unified legal system.

This centralist movement also played an important role in other countries. Since this was an element in the competition between the different royal houses and their territories, its success was of vital importance to the state and resistance to it had to be crushed. This movement failed in the Netherlands. The question is, why did this happen?. Urban resistance was not confined to these regions. Wherever markets developed, people attempted to free themselves from the plethora of traditional feudal rights and looked for support from the sovereign or the central government which in return for the promised tax contributions transferred the rights of the local aristocracy to the city authorities. This meant that in future they would be able to decide for themselves how taxes should be collected, as long as they ensured that the regular contributions were paid. While the sovereign and the cities formed a united front against the nobility they also had opposing interests. The one wanted money and the other had to pay it. This relationship resembled the old feudal system, where the vassal, having received certain privileges from the liege-lord, began to regard this privilege as a right and started up for himself as soon as he was able. This centrifugal danger repeated itself but now with the cities as the unfaithful subjects which, whenever they got the chance, distanced themselves from state authority. As we have seen, this kind of revolt occurred in different places when towards the end of the Middle Ages the degree of centralization was still minimal in comparison to the degree of commercialization; these revolts were most successful where there was the greatest difficulty in maintaining centralization. This was certainly the case with the Italian city states, the North German Hanseatic cities and those of the Low Countries; the developments were parallel until the Low Countries combined to rebel and laid the grounds for an independent state, which although often threatened and twice conquered, was to endure for many years.

Why did this succeed here and not elsewhere? The answer is clear. The German states, it is true, formed a competitive and cooperative unit, but they were too disparate to form a territorial defensive union as the Dutch cities had done; moreover, their territory was easier to defend and difficult to attack through the natural or artificial flooding of strategic areas. Consequently Germany retained its autonomous republican free ports until late in the nineteenth century when they were finally incorporated into the German empire. The crucial difference with the Italian cities is another story. These city states also lay further apart than the Dutch cities, but more importantly there was no common enemy and no single city state predominated. Because of this, rival cities did not join together to form a larger state association and they kept their freedom of trade until the nineteenth century when they too were incorporated into the new unity of the Italian state.

These two conditions did prevail in Holland. The enemy was Spain, while internally Holland was the dominant element and 'convinced' the other parties to participate through the use of open or covert threats, and in one case with the use of arms. This last was the city of Groningen, situated on the periphery of the Dutch Republic and which had actually set its sights on the German empire but which was forced, with a minimal amount of bloodshed, to participate in the Union. The degree of participation and integration remained extremely modest. In fact, the Union formed a cooperation in which the autonomy of the parts was maintained. The barrier to entry was therefore low and this greatly facilitated the foundation of what can best be termed a confederation.

Last but by no means least of these explanations for the success of the Republic was the weakness of the enemy. The barrier to integration of the Habsburg areas was high, as was the difficulty experienced in the struggle towards centralization. This was true of the Austrian-Habsburg areas, but even more so of the Spanish branch, which lay dispersed across Europe. Moreover, the territory of the Union, as already mentioned, consisted of marshy fens which were easily accessible commercially but not militarily, as many an attacking army had already experienced before the Spanish Don Alva invaded the land and was forced to leave empty-handed. Thus began a period of success which, at least until the French period, can best be compared to that of the Swiss confederation which, due partly to its geographical situation, had already joined in resistance against the centralizing ambitions of external powers.

However successful the Union was, as a unit it was barely a state at all, the creation of which had been the original endeavour and had been given symbolic expression as a lion with seven arrows in one of its paws.[16] This symbol of 'unity makes power' referred to the legend of the Persian king Darius, who is supposed to have impressed upon his sons that the bundle was stronger than the individual arrows. The proposals bear witness to this. Although composed of representatives of cities and regions, the Union was to make decisions by majority vote without the complication of consultation. In this way it was hoped to levy a central and uniform tax on all members of the Republic. That this never occurred should come as no surprise. A common external threat can form a condition for state formation, but unlike direct conquest the governing principle is never the interest of the whole but always that of the parts. States which are constructed in this way remain weak and most disappear or are forced from a federal onto a more centralist course through internal or external opposition. This latter scenario applies to the Netherlands, with an exception to the rule being Switzerland.

When it was finally agreed, the Union of Utrecht did not include these centralized measures. Instead of a majority vote the principle of unanimity was adopted, which involved consulting the regional authorities; these in turn were made accountable to the local authorities. The decision-making process was thus slow. This tardiness gave rise to the expression 'at the eleven-and-thirtiest' – referring to the province of Friesland. Eleven cities and thirty districts had to give their authorization to their representatives in the regional councils which in turn had to give their authorization to the representatives in the States General before a decision (which had been accepted as a proposal considerably earlier) could be adopted. After this process the decision had to go through the same procedure in all seven provinces.

The same fate awaited proposals for the regulation of what could anachronistically be termed import and export duties, thus affecting the formation of the internal market. These were known as 'convoys and licences', the first of which was a levy – originally linked to the protection of vessels carrying imports or exports at sea – and the second a sort of licensing system for trading with enemy markets. Both systems, which differed in each region and even from city to city, were to be brought under a central organization, so that on the one hand a kind of economic frontier would be formed, while on the other hand the internal market would be freed from having to deal with the many different systems. This centralization was extremely important because internal competition continually forced tariffs to be lowered and trade with even a direct enemy was tolerated. This is the reason why in this case economic unity preceded unity of 'state'. But this did not succeed either. It is true that the proposals were accepted on paper, but through the absence of a sufficiently powerful central authority the external threat was not great enough to directly override individual interests. It is remarkable, but true. While armies were fighting and people were being killed, trade with the enemy continued with the painfully true excuse that 'If I don't do it, someone else will'.

Trade can thus be described as 'free', but not 'liberal' *avant la lettre*. This description is also misleading. It is true that in this period between the old feudal and the new centralist system trade freed itself from previous barriers, while new ones did not yet exist or were ineffective. This trade was, nevertheless, not part of a free market. It was free in a general way, and formed a mixed bag of trade and piracy. It was a piracy in which the Dutch competed almost as fiercely with each other as with others. And like the other privateering cities, although less catastrophically, the Dutch cities were defeated by the upcoming states and their protected mercantilism based on a free internal market. In the seventeenth and eighteenth centuries the structure of the Dutch Republic hardly changed. It remained united in a kind of internal discord; a weak, confederate state structure, which with the absence of a clear central authority could scarcely be considered a focus of identification around which its constituents could base their activities. Direct commercial self-interest dominated and, accompanying this, a society based on negotiation. The much-lauded tolerance – in which the Republic or rather the individual cities distinguished themselves and which was expressed in a gradual development away from direct persecution of those who thought differently, and towards the care of orphans, and imprisonment rather than the maiming of law-breakers – should be seen in the first place from the perspective of the commercial elite. Its principal interest lay not in repressive state control but in the free traffic of goods and its inseparable corollary, the free traffic of persons and ideas. Moreover, because of the nature of its activities, this upper echelon was more dependent on the way city populations earned their livelihood than aristocratic elites elsewhere. The fates of the upper classes and common folk were economically and otherwise interwoven so that the perceived self-interest of the one was also that of the other. This emphasis on interweaving interests did not prevent the rise of a moral or a more spontaneous movement towards tolerance and mutual consideration. Nevertheless, this impetus apparently only began to take effect at a later date. Relations in the Republic in the sixteenth and seventeenth centuries were not particularly sensitive. They were to become so, not among the upper classes, but among the bourgeois middle classes in the second half of the eighteenth century, and they differed little from developments in other countries.

In the nineteenth century relations changed. The authority of the state became centralized in the early part of the century, although to a moderate degree, but the relatively egalitarian relations remained. This period saw the establishment of the free internal market with the gradual disbanding of the many internal levies and the establishment of a customs service based on the French model but functioning more along the lines of the English model. After the secession of the Belgian southern provinces which had become part of the new Dutch kingdom after the defeat of France, the old trading interests began to come to the fore again. In line with this policy the customs service followed a liberal course similar to that in Britain, although without the fear of letting in disease. 'Trade-friendly' control continued into the twentieth century and became the kind of characteristic cultural trait that distinguished the Netherlands from other countries. Nowhere, except here, could guidelines for customs officials dictate that trade should be obstructed by as few state controls as possible.[17]

Germany – legalistic centralism

Up to now, the findings have shown how long it takes and how difficult it is to establish a free internal market within an area with a central authority. The Dutch model illustrates that these difficulties can be insurmountable if the central authority is especially weak.

An example against which the accuracy of this thesis can be tested is the formation of state and market in Germany. This Central European country was the last of the major powers to appear on the European stage. The explanation for this is again connected with geographical conditions. Of the three major states, Germany is the least blessed with natural frontiers. As far as these exist they form an area whose size makes state formation far more difficult than in other countries. History shows this to be true. While the central authority increased its hold in England and France in the sixteenth and seventeenth centuries, this proved unattainable for the German territories. The Habsburg empire disintegrated and the Peace of Westphalia that ended the Thirty Years' War in 1648 left the area ravaged and impoverished. During the following century a new integration movement emerged, this time centred on the Prussian territories of the Hohenzollerns, with Berlin as the focus. Relations in Prussia's periphery were based on large-scale landholding and a limited degree of internal commercialization. The result was a major social distinction between the aristocracy and the remainder of the population, who lived, particularly in the north-east of Prussia, in a contorted, 'medieval' dependence on the nobility. Prussian expansionism was therefore an authoritarian military movement which, unlike France in that period, was not supported by an extensive hierarchy of civil servants. It was actually alienated from the bourgeois culture of professions and commerce, and even tended to despise that culture.

This was the general situation that existed in many German cities where, on a small scale, the influence of the middle classes remained limited and that of the nobility, extensive. Differences in power levels of this order indicate a low degree of commercialization, which in its turn indicates a market as fragmented as political Germany was itself, perhaps even more so. Even within the expanding Prussia of the late eighteenth century, trade had to contend with a myriad medieval and imperial tolls, augmented by numerous initiatives introduced by later and more local authorities.

This situation soon changed. Under the French occupation, various German states were amalgamated and the central authority was increased within these coalitions. One result of this outcome was that, in these states, initiatives were taken to form a free internal market, including the centralization and unification of taxes and the organization of a civil service to implement this.

Prussia was among the powers that defeated France, but even after this defeat and the revival of numerous German states which had been amalgamated, the movement continued and expanded into a market formation process which was to spread across numerous frontiers and cover much of Germany. In 1834 a majority of German states decided to form a customs union, known in German as the Zollverein. It was to last for some thirty years, to be followed by the North German Confederation and later by the new German Empire.[18] It was highly successful from the beginning. Despite economic differences and conflicts between the large-scale landholders in north-east Prussia producing grain for export who, despite their natural conservatism, were inclined towards liberalism and the small-scale industries of the southern states, it proved possible to unite these diverse interests. The result was an increased productivity all round and a growing internal market.

From this perspective the Zollverein appears to be the first exception to the rule that the market always comes after the state. In Germany it was apparently the healthy market-oriented view that eventually defeated the small-minded divisive interests. It was a victory for the bourgeois market with its two weapons, negotiation and mutual trust, against the aristocratic army with its one-sided perspective of order and obedience. The conditions were favourable. The French occupation had laid the foundation. The German territories had the same language and culture and the economic differences were not insurmountable. One of the states involved was dominant and capable of using the prospect of punishment or reward to coerce states that hesitated. Moreover, and this was new, models now existed for the creation of an internal market, showing the tremendous advantages to be gained. There was increasing knowledge about state and market and German scholars learned from their illustrious French and British predecessors. Yet there was another important factor. Even though the conditions were indeed propitious, it was eventually military force that turned Germany into a single market.

The creation of the customs union certainly had the backing of non-military bourgeois organizations. It served their economic activities and the union reflected their ideal of an end to the political division and the formation of a German state in the areas of German language and culture. Nevertheless, it was not they but the Prussians who, on their own terms, were to realize the ideal. The whole endeavour was under Prussian leadership from the very beginning, not limiting itself to presenting proposals and passing resolutions. While Prussia may not have dictated events, it nevertheless threatened to leave the union on more than one occasion to form a coalition with other territories, confronting opponents with the prospect of economic and military isolation and so, in the end, forcing them to play safe. In reality, the give and take was mutual. Prussia compromised, by adjusting its liberal system, against its own immediate economic interests, in favour of emerging industries of the other territories. Prussia was eager, moved not so much by economics and culture as by political motives which remained sagaciously unspoken: the emperor and chancellor's hidden agenda which the other states awaited in anticipation with a mixture of obedience and resistance.

Gradually, Prussia's aims became clear. The union was organized on a system of unanimous voting and the resulting lethargic pace led Prussia to propose changing the system for one of majority voting. In itself, this move towards centralization had the support of bourgeois groups. In fact, after the revolution in Paris in February of 1848 they took the initiative themselves. Their first achievement was the installation of a constitution in Prussia. It introduced a diet with an upper chamber appointed by the king himself and a lower chamber elected by a restricted electorate, thus keeping the level of democracy low.

However, in a wider context, just as previously and elsewhere, citizens attempted to extend their own influence and the unity of exchange and order. Throughout the country elections were held for the national German diet at Frankfurt am Main. After a year of debate it was decided to institute a hereditary German empire, excluding Austria. The throne of this small-scale Germany was offered to the Prussian king. He refused it: he had no wish to 'pick up a crown from the gutter'. He wished to rule, and opposed liberal, parliamentary monarchy. This refusal proved too much for the fragile bourgeois offensive. Fear of Prussian militarism and their own lack of arms had led them to make the offer. The same reasons prevented them from taking their own initiative, as the Prussians had anticipated. The way was now open to end the irritating division of the customs union and to create German unity internally and externally by force. And indeed this is what happened. In a series of short wars convincingly won by the Prussian army, the North German Confederation was founded, followed by the new German Empire after the defeat of France in 1871.

German bourgeois liberalism and nationalism had clearly failed. Many supported the military authoritarian nationalism which had shown itself to be superior. It was to characterize the German situation. A centralist state was set up based in Berlin, although some functions were delegated to the former states or associations of these units, thus retaining something of the old confederate Zollverein. As a result the German state was less hierarchically centralist than in France, although the similarities were considerable. Government powers were, however, just as authoritarian, with the significant difference being that the German 'order' was more legalistic and formal while in France it was more opportunist and calculated. An interesting example of the gradual differences, which also applies to the Netherlands and Britain, concerns the respective legal systems, particularly the criminal justice systems.

Differences in the judicial apparatus

The centralization and unification of the judicial apparatus runs parallel to the creation of a centrally organized police force and a free internal market. A central authority's first concern is to establish a monopoly on violence and on taxation – the latter in a rudimentary form – followed only later by the other functions.[19] This development in France is the most well known. Here, the revolution led to the replacement of the patchwork of local and regional laws by the famous codes aimed at establishing unity and equality under the law and an end to aristocratic and other privileges which had increasingly been perceived as arbitrary. The scope and system of the judicial apparatus expanded, thus increasing the control it exerted. Meanwhile the repressive powers were tempered. Punishments became more lenient and less consideration was given to a person's social position and more to so-called mitigating circumstances.

The same development occurred in Germany. Again, the direct influence of the French occupation, and various later domestic initiatives, led to the introduction in the nineteenth century of several German legal codes with similar functions. Unity came only after the establishment of the empire and a single criminal law was promulgated for the entire country. This German legal code was, in general, based on the French system, although with variations. It clearly reflected the unique circumstances of German unification and Prussian domination – aspects that are still revealed in today's system. A significant difference is the principle in Germany that every crime must be prosecuted. The French system differs in that the state judicial apparatus is not forced to prosecute if there are convincing reasons not to do so; for example, that the punishment might be out of proportion to the crime, the futility of a crime, mitigating circumstances, changes in public feelings about the law or simply a question of setting priorities for the use of limited resources.

The difference is interesting and seems in the first place to suggest there would be differences in the reliability of the various judicial and police machineries. In Germany this reliability was clearly limited, leading to the preference for a tough implementation of the law; in France the level of reliability was higher and the law was made subject in particular cases to the judgment of the judicial authorities, with all the room for manoeuvre that this provided. It is probably right to relate these discrepancies to social contrasts and disparity in general. Differences between regions and classes in France were perhaps more significant than those in

Britain, or especially Holland, but they were less significant than in Germany, where the compulsory nature of law could be moderated through negotiation and mutual trust. Nevertheless, it would be wrong in a comparison such as this to interpret the French perspective exclusively in this light. The wider scope allowed in the French law was accompanied by a certain trust by the population in the judicial apparatus, although this probably also involved the trust of the central authority in its servants. Unlike Germany, France could boast a civil service that had developed over the centuries and now formed a relatively obedient means of control. As a result, the freedom of manoeuvre of the judicial apparatus was in fact the freedom of manoeuvre of direct central authority, thereby serving the interests of the state.

This was a typically French situation. A flexibility that could be defended on grounds of humanity, in reality, served the interests of the state. Indeed, the French state formed a focus of identification for which throughout the nineteenth century ever more peripheral groups felt a bond but at the same time, because of its clear dominance, it also formed an object of fear and resistance.

In Germany the situation was different. The system of compulsory prosecution reflected a lower level of mutual trust; or rather, it reflected the relatively sharp contrasts between population groups and between these and the central authorities. As a result, the country developed a legal code which was harsh but which put in place an authoritarian instrument that guaranteed, however inadequately, against arbitrariness and vendetta, thereby helping to counter the fear of these spectres.

This was the origin of the German authoritarian ethos, which for two reasons led to the proverbial obedience of Germans: the fear of punishment and the fear of chaos and terror. The subsequent history of the German empire and later events entrenched this attitude, so that it is now a typically German characteristic. It is also reflected in the judicial systematization and dogmatic thinking which others find constrained and odd. This is also true of France, where the civil service hierarchy serves the function carried out in Germany by the law. As we have seen, however much they may differ, both countries have a hierarchic, centralist structure and mentality. The French structure is more opportunist or calculating, while the German structure is more legalist or formalist in style.

Astonishment concerning the German system extends particularly to Britain and Holland. In fact, Dutch law does not incorporate compulsory prosecution. In line with its egalitarian and moderate centralist system it is actually the judicial apparatus which determines its own room for manoeuvre. Recent decades have seen this scope extended increasingly and the rule is now that a prosecution is only pursued if it is considered necessary.

France and Germany are in turn surprised by the relative flexibility of the Dutch system and they criticize the Netherlands for its apparent inability to take firm action. This complaint plays a role, for example, in the coordination of drug policies, although, as we shall discuss below, it remains to be seen which approach is the more effective.

Britain is a separate case in this respect. The codification of Europe's legal systems which the French occupation instituted through the systematization, egalitarianism and centralization across the Continent, never reached Britain. Nevertheless, the British legal system is also uniform. This uniformity was not defined by law in the eighteenth and nineteenth centuries; it developed in the course of the centuries, initially through an accumulated body of precedent and later through more and more statutes, although not in a necessarily systemized manner. Consequently the British system has never had to form a statement of principle on the question of compulsory prosecution, although in practice it can be said not to apply. Moreover, and this is typical of the British system, the decision to prosecute has not been the responsibility of a separate body, but rather that of the police and the general public in exercising the right to take individuals to court, a form used only in rare cases on the Continent. Clearly, despite the increasing influence of the Continental System on Britain, it still remains different in structure and reflects the early centralization of the state and its unwillingness to intervene in the comparatively egalitarian system.

The characteristic German system, discussed here in the light of an international comparison, also finds expression in the protection of its economic frontiers and its national customs service. This service extends back to the beginnings of the Zollverein, originally based on the French model but imbued with the Prussian ethos. This worried other countries at the time. Holland felt especially threatened; Rotterdam was becoming a major harbour for the

German hinterland through which it supplied raw materials from what was then the Dutch East Indies. The attitude was ambivalent. On the one hand, the Dutch hoped to profit from the growing industry of the German economic bloc; on the other hand, high import tariffs threatened to eliminate Dutch competition. What should they do? Dutch attitudes and interests were eloquently expressed in reactions to Germany's violation of the sacred principle of free trade. They aligned themselves with the French camp, while it was generally believed in Holland that Britain's free trade policy would eventually triumph. Nevertheless, it was undeniable that 'with regard to their rights, their taxes and their material interests [the Zollverein] had made 23 million Germans citizens of the same state'.[20] Some thought it would be wise to join, thereby counteracting the disadvantageous effects while also profiting from the advantages of the large market. In the end that option was not taken.

> It would have meant accepting a system which trade has always considered the most despicable, the greatest enemy, a system of privilege, of high tariffs and exclusions. We would find that the Prussian customs officials – Dutch civil servants would in fact simply become Prussian officials in spirit and system – would become as irritating as the French were ... high tariffs, painstaking revision, weighing, measuring, irritating, moreover, once introduced, outside products will become much too expensive.

The conclusion is clear. As a reasonable compromise the Dutch government decided to enter a commercial treaty with the Zollverein. In 1839 agreements with Prussia and the other signatories led to lower tariffs for Dutch trade. This solution typified the Dutch view of trade and negotiation in which Holland showed itself more experienced than the Germans; it soon became apparent to the Germans that they had concluded an agreement for Dutch colonial sugar which was extremely advantageous to the Dutch. Somewhat taken aback, they spoke of the Dutch as '*den geschickt taktierenden holländischen Unterhändlern*'.

In this way, Holland was able to manoeuvre between the great powers, whose mutual rivalries had to some extent been the reason for its emergence in the first place and was to remain so for some time. European rivalry had led to open conflict twice in the twentieth century and all those involved were left exhausted. They faced the question whether, after centuries of competition between states and markets, there might not be another way.

3

THE ORIGINS OF THE
EUROPEAN UNION

In 1957, more than ten years after the end of the Second World War,
a number of states joined forces to form a new alliance. These states
resolved to replace the economic boundaries between them with
common external boundaries and to establish an internal free
market, the European Community. Initially, the implementation of
their resolution was an uphill struggle, but in recent years the
process has gained momentum and it seems likely that the free
market will be realized, *grosso modo*, before the end of the twentieth
century, having taken a total of less than fifty years.

The slow rate of progress may be a source of irritation for some.
However, comparing the process with earlier attempts at similar
objectives, it now seems on course to succeed, namely, in the
establishment of an internal free market with external economic
boundaries; a common market to be established before rather than
after a common state. For the first time, the process was not
prompted by war or by the threat of violence, but by enlightened
self-interest of the states involved who had finally realized that a
large internal free market would be beneficial, and had allowed
centripetal forces to dominate over centrifugal forces.

However, this is not the case this time either. Soon after the
Second World War various initiatives were developed to bring about
the unification of Europe as a reaction to the evident catastrophic
consequences of disunity. To a certain extent this process was similar
to that which had taken place after the French occupation of
German territory and had lasted until the mid-nineteenth century.
However, there were obvious differences, which made the conditions for European unification less favourable than they had been
for German unification, and it was evident that even those conditions had not been sufficiently favourable. Nationalism had been

46

the driving force behind German unification. Although Germany lacked unity of authority and trade, there was a certain unity of language, and therefore a unity of culture and history, albeit fragmented. The postwar movement towards European integration lacked this nationalistic impetus. It was based on internationalism and federalism, and although there were those who argued that there was a European culture, this identity was too vague in reality and missed a clear counterpoint to take the place of nationalism.

Another difference was that German unification had been economically and militarily dominated by the Prussians. Although this military aristocratic hegemony formed a threat to unification, it was also an integrative force which served to bridge the impasse caused by discord among the population. The European unification movement lacked this sort of internal domination. The peoples involved were a heterogeneous group and moreover, most had little sympathy with aristocratic military aspirations. This was hardly surprising. The aristocracy's field of influence had diminished for a variety of reasons, not least because of the course of recent military history. Furthermore, the wounds that had been opened by battle had only just started to heal. The European endeavour was therefore strongly pacifist, not militaristic. It was not directed towards a redress of the old loyalties, nor towards their extension, but towards their abolition. Although this was a noble endeavour, it soon became apparent that a lot more was required to bring about some form of cooperation between nations, particularly since they had been unable to cooperate in the past. Nevertheless, the unification process had been initiated. The conditions for this lay elsewhere, namely in the new balance of power that emerged after the war, and although it may seem contradictory, this balance of power made the European Community a confirmation of earlier processes of market and state formation, at least during the first phase of unification – from 1945 to around 1980.

THE FIRST PHASE: THE EUROPEAN COMMUNITY AS A SEGMENT OF THE AMERICAN WORLD MARKET

The most important condition for the formation of the European Economic Community was not strictly European but European-American, with the United States as the dominant party. This country, which has not featured in the discussion until now, was established towards the end of the eighteenth century, when a number of British colonies joined forces to break free from the motherland. Their unification was a success. During the course of the nineteenth century the country developed into a federation, which brought the separatist South under control during the Civil War. It subsequently extended its state monopolies on violence, taxation and jurisdiction and the United States started to defend its external economic and military boundaries. This American internal market was geographically extensive and the country developed into an economic power with a concomitant military potential which manifested itself increasingly during the course of the twentieth century. This first became apparent during the First World War. The United States had initially maintained its traditional neutrality but had later become involved, forcing a breakthrough in the seemingly endless trench war. Their involvement was based on political and military motives and reflected the bond that still existed between the old motherland and the American social elite. The economic development of the United States not only made the country powerful but also vulnerable, because the country had an increasing number of interests abroad which had to be protected. The protection of their interests by means of direct military intervention was short-lived, with the country withdrawing from Europe soon after the end of the First World War. Their task was complete and the majority of Americans believed that an extended sojourn in the European snake-pit, with its age-old feuds, would be a waste of money and human resources, from which no clear benefits could be expected. Nevertheless, they extended their economic ties with certain European states; for example, with Britain, but particularly with Germany. While the 'triumphant' European countries concentrated on their demands for reparations, American companies invested in the new Germany and established a wide variety of joint ventures. However, the Great Depression put an end to this community of interests. All sides withdrew to within their own boundaries and war broke out again. Once again, the United States initially remained neutral, but when the country itself was attacked a difficult decision became the only option. The United States became involved in another war beyond its borders and once again its efforts were successful. However, American policy after the second victory was very different from its policy after the first victory. Before the war was over America had resolved to aid impoverished Europe by providing extensive support and restoring economic activity. This scheme to provide support on a grand scale, the Marshall Plan, was intended to eradicate the age-old discord and proved to be in the interests of both Europe and the United States.[1]

The American and Russian monopolists

America's resolve was strengthened, rather than prompted, by its growing rivalry with a new superpower – the Soviet Union. These two superpowers had fought more or less side by side to win the war.

The Soviet Union was the successor to the Russian tsarist empire, which had ruled large parts of Eastern Europe and Central Asia. The role of this peripheral empire was far from insignificant for the rest of Europe, partly because it divided Europe into three parts, with Germany in the middle, which meant that the latter would always have to fight on two fronts. At the beginning of the twentieth century, the workers and peasants, backed by rebel army units, had put an end to the tsarist regime. However, this changed neither the balance of power nor the tense relations that had existed for centuries and which were partly geographically determined. The new regime therefore maintained the traditional centralized authoritarian state – in spite of their radical socialist rhetoric – and continued to form coalitions, either with Germany or with one or more of the Western European states. The power politics of the communist regime were initially applauded by radical intellectuals in the West, who later denounced the system *en masse*. Indeed, judging by Western standards, the regime was barbaric. To a certain extent this repressive system was necessary to maintain unity and to raise production to a satisfactory level so that the Soviet Union could defend itself against its enemies. In other words, the integration threshold was high, higher than in Germany, and a powerful central regime was required to ensure that the centripetal forces would dominate the centrifugal forces.

This balance of power remained when Germany was defeated and the Soviet Union and the United States met face to face for the first time at the river Elbe. These were the two most powerful superpowers, but the differences in economic and military strength were enormous, as were the differences in state structure and dominant ideology. The Soviet Union was the weaker of the two. It had a greater historical right to be suspicious and it used the opportunity to fortify itself. The Americans reacted swiftly. They entrenched themselves, even though they had initially intended to withdraw, and within a short period Germany, and later Europe, was divided into two camps which regarded outsiders across the globe with a suspicion. The Cold War had begun.

These transformations were remarkable for the extent of their influence on global affairs and the magnitude and power of the military potential, which posed an all-encompassing threat. However, at the same time, they were a direct continuation of earlier processes of market and state formation, in which competitive tension between states had led to the formation of ever larger alliances, by threat or by deployment of force. This process was particularly evident in Eastern Europe, where a new military and economic alliance had been formed. This alliance was monopolized by the Soviet Union, which had not only had the opportunity to do so, having emerged victorious from the war, but also felt driven to do so, on account of the new rivalry. This new state and market, the Warsaw Pact and Comecon, was characterized by a highly centralized structure similar to that of the dominant party, where the economy was controlled by the state rather than by 'market forces'. This state-controlled command economy was legitimized by arguing that the system would make amends for the injustices of the free market economy. However, in truth it was the frailty of the market, rather than its injustice, which necessitated top-down state control of productivity in order to maintain a competitive edge. This high level of state control is reminiscent of the situation in other countries, albeit in a more moderate form, in which the state controls the economy in order to catch up with its rivals. This was the case in ancient and modern China, but also in Japan, France, Britain (during the mercantilist–absolutist period), Germany (during the nineteenth century and the first half of the twentieth century) and in most other countries that tried to gain strategic power.

The United States was no exception to this rule. During the nineteenth century this modern day champion of the free market was a mercantilist state, which not only protected its own internal market against the European great powers but also those of the entire American continent. This policy changed when the balance of power shifted. The United States displayed its power by serving its own interests with free trade, as Britain had done in the past, and by becoming the self-appointed military and monetary controller of the 'global free market' after the Second World War. This global free market may be seen as the American internal free market in the making. This changing of the guard between Britain and the United

States is probably symbolized best by the Bretton Woods Agreements, named after the hotel in New Hampshire in the United States where they were signed. These agreements were reached in 1944 and were implemented two years later. They led to the establishment of the International Monetary Fund, for which the dollar and not the pound was the standard unit of currency. This heralded a period of increased market and state expansion in the West, paralleling developments in Eastern Europe. The American monopoly was actually less coercive than its Russian counterpart and, as we have seen, the United States was the stronger of the two and had less to fear, particularly in geographical–strategic terms. As a result, the unification of what became the Western Bloc was largely based on negotiation and mutual trust. Nevertheless, the interdependence here was equally biased towards the United States which called all the shots and, although the power of decision of the Western European states was not openly opposed, it was certainly contained.

NATO and OEEC/OECD

The establishment of the North Atlantic Treaty Organization (NATO) in 1949 was of paramount importance to these relations. The member states participated in this organization voluntarily and on the basis of formal equality. In truth, however, the member states placed their defence forces at the disposal of the American President. They thereby relinquished an important part of their sovereignty without obtaining democratic powers of authorization.[2]

NATO was the military counterpart of the Warsaw Pact, which had actually been established six years later. On the economic front the parallel was less obvious, although an integrative process had been initiated. This was extended to a revision of the international monetary system, which was swiftly followed by the implementation of the Marshall Plan, a striking example of what enlightened self-interest could achieve within this system of relations. The object of this large-scale economic relief plan was to revitalize the European economy and to prevent the United States from slipping into a postwar depression. The Marshall Plan had initially included the Soviet Union, but the latter had refused to take part. By then, tension had mounted and the Soviet Union had chosen to make up lost ground under its own steam. This refusal accelerated the escalation of tension, but also reduced the complexity of the situation, which was considerable due to the diversity of the states involved and the rivalry between them. The solution was simple: the states would become part of a single market, which would not be isolated but would form part of an Atlantic market that would be the economic complement of NATO. Both the economic and the military alliance would, in turn, form part of an even larger system, the global free market, the 'Forum Americanum', which would be protected by the global free state, the 'Imperium Americanum'. This world order was a dream, a vague concept generally presented in fragmented and diplomatically embellished forms. However, at the same time it gave an indication of the direction in which the postwar process was headed. Victory had been a prerequisite for this process, which was spurred on by the mounting competitive tension between East and West with the 'American plan for Europe' forming part of this process.

The pressure applied by the Americans on the Western European states proved successful where before centuries of reciprocal rivalry had failed. They had all been defeated and the new monopolist had agreed to provide relief, on condition that the states would attempt to achieve economic integration. The establishment of the Organization for European Economic Cooperation (OEEC) in 1948 was the first significant step taken in this direction. This organization is now known as the Organization for Economic Cooperation and Development (OECD) which has its seat in Paris. It included the Western European states and almost all other states which played a significant part in the Forum Americanum, indicative of the broader context of European integration.

ECCS and EDC

The second step was limited to the European arena. In 1951 the European Community for Coal and Steel (ECCS) was established. Under pressure from the Americans and with the consent of European politicians who advocated a pragmatic variant of European federalist idealism, heavy industry in Western Europe was placed under communal control.[3] This put an end to the industrial discord between certain states – particularly France and Germany – and was a prerequisite for the recovery of the European economy in general and for the arms industry in particular. The Benelux countries formed part of the ECCS, as did Italy, but Britain remained outside. This country still saw itself as the world power it had once been, and presented itself as a champion of the new world order alongside the

United States. The British maintained this aloofness for a long time, causing delays in the European integration process, particularly in geographical terms. The island kingdom was eventually to suffer the most. Its age-old economic lead gradually disappeared and it was relegated to the rearguard of the European pack, and not only in economic terms.

The British remained aloof towards European integration when the resolution to establish a European Defence Community (EDC) was passed. All the member states of the ECCS participated in this organization. These plans are highly significant for the present discourse. Until then, it had been argued that there was no place for a European defence organization, because NATO had fulfilled this role since the war. NATO alliance was dominated by the new monopolist, the United States, which protected the member states against external threats and, although this has never been articulated, also offered protection against states which wanted to break away from the alliance, thus becoming a potential threat themselves. Therefore, the question remains: what prompted the resolution to establish the EDC? The answer is that although the power of the United States was impressive, it was rarely ever put to effective use. It applied its power surplus with a certain restraint, thus disguising the discrepancy between its own military and economic potential and that of the European states. Moreover, the true discrepancy was toned down and, as a result, France tried to repair its shattered national pride by distancing itself from NATO and by manufacturing its own atomic weapon as a symbol of its sovereignty. Even before, France had tried to regain its national pride via the European Defence Community, an alliance of European states, with, following the German defeat, a distinctly French flavour. The United States' reaction to the French endeavour for greater independence was not that of a jealous monopolist. Although French ambitions were a source of irritation, their endeavour was not seen as a dangerous centrifugal force, nor as a threat to the alliance and to America itself. The Americans viewed this from a different angle. They saw the EDC as the European wing of NATO, which not only allowed the alliance to harness the German potential in an acceptable manner but would also be an incentive for greater economic integration in combination with the ECCS. The United States was not concerned about the exact ingredients of the balance of power. Whatever French and European ambitions might develop, the Americans had economic and military forces at their disposal which

– for the politically foreseeable future – would remain superior to any other. Moreover, the plans were mere resolutions and it was therefore uncertain whether or not they would be implemented.

The French eventually balked at the final jump and the plans were never implemented. Tragically, their hesitation was the result of their colonial–imperial legacy, which had to be defended and did not tally with their European ambitions. Apparently, the French valued their colonial ambitions more than their continental ambitions and, as a result, they failed on both fronts. France was forced to face the fact that it was a modest European state, like its neighbours, and had trouble accepting this status, as had the British.

The EDC fiasco shows that the odds were against the establishment of a European state during this period. The reasons have already been reviewed above. The threat of war posed by the Soviet Union was the strongest centripetal force or incentive for integration at the time. This was directed towards the United States and not towards Europe. This rule was repeatedly reinforced: when the threat of war escalated, the European states turned to their monopolist, one at a time. However, whenever the threat diminished, they communally lamented their one-sided dependence and vainly resolved to change this state of affairs. The EDC fiasco was a lesson which the European states chose not to learn, because it underscored their dependence on the United States, bruised their national pride and was a painful reminder of the past.

One of the main consequences of the fiasco was that the Federal Republic of (West) Germany, formed in 1949, did not join the European alliance but became a direct member of NATO. Formally, this meant that the country regained its military respectability, albeit with certain limitations, and bolstered the Atlantic military alliance, because there was no other European alternative. However, the fiasco was greeted with a sigh of relief by many of the smaller EDC member states, particularly the Netherlands. A resounding 'no' to the EDC would have been unwise, considering the balance of power and the desire for European integration, but a 'yes' seemed equally perilous. The Dutch had reservations about a strong bond with France, because it conflicted with their ties with the United States and Britain, and because it was seen as essentially and emotionally irreconcilable with the international balance of power to which the Netherlands owed its existence. The French had temporarily solved the problem when they balked at the final jump, leaving the Dutch beyond blame both on the Continent and overseas.

In subsequent years the existence of a field of tension between French ambitions and Dutch interests was repeatedly confirmed. This was fuelled by the continuity of policy, but also by that of the actual balance of power, which may not have been subject to long-term analysis but did effect the succession of *ad hoc* decisions.

The founding of the European Community

The silence after the storm of the EDC fiasco was short-lived. In an effort to save face, a military alliance, the Western European Union (WEU), was established. Britain was a member of this organization, which entailed only a few obligations. A far less ambitious plan subsequently became the main subject of diplomatic intercourse between the states: economic integration. The European states successfully took up the thread of the Marshall Plan, the OECD and the ECCS. In 1957 the Treaty of Rome was signed, marking the birth of the European Community. The Community was a synthesis of three intergovernmental cooperative organizations: the earlier ECCS, the European Nuclear Community and the European Economic Community. As is now well known, the Community's main objective was to establish an internal free market within the foreseeable future.[4] The success of this endeavour to date does not negate the state-to-market order of events which has been argued here. Even though the states have not been forced to form the Community and have formally retained their autonomy, this first step towards establishing a free market was indirectly a product of American supremacy. After the war the United States had forced the European states to work together in ways in which they had never previously done. This cooperation was limited primarily to the market, because the most important function of state, the monopoly on violence, had already been regulated in a different alliance.

Germany and France

The conditions imposed by the United States did not exclude other favourable conditions, such as the development of European federalism which was prompted by the danger of European disunity. A more significant factor, however, was the role played by the new Federal Republic of Germany. Unlike after the First World War, the Community gave the defeated country the opportunity to rehabilitate itself and to recover lost ground. West Germany was eager to participate and soon became a driving force prepared to reach a compromise on any issue, provided it contributed to progress. West Germany suppressed all forms of limiting self-interest and dented pride, and burdened itself with a disproportionate share of the costs.

West Germany, which soon stood at the head of the pack in economic terms but still lacked status, had a counterpart: France.[5] Almost as a matter of course, the Community's bureaucratic apparatus was modelled on French hierarchic centralism. The diplomatic etiquette was also based on the reserved, French, *hautain* style, a remnant of the former aristocratic 'aloofness' which had been adopted by the new ruling classes. Language was one of the most characteristic features of French influence on the European system. Although the member states were, in principle, equal, the lingua franca of the Community was French, and those who did not speak the language were expected to attend a crash course as soon as possible. France's economic position was far less convincing however. The country had engaged in lengthy vacillation before joining the Community. The French feared that they would be inundated with foreign products and that their country would become a European backwater if their protected tariffs were adjusted to keep pace with European standards. Their fears were not completely unfounded, because the Germans outdid the French in their ability to compete with other producers on the world market. The Germans would thus benefit from a more liberal form of competition. Nevertheless, the French eventually surrendered, the main reason being the Community's agricultural policy. France was the largest producer of agricultural products and it had done its utmost to protect this sector through high import duties and high export subsidies. These interests formed the basis of the French demands. The French wanted Europe to adopt their agricultural policy so that, on the one hand, farming and related activities would remain protected and, on the other, the costs of protection would be shared. The French also demanded that high external tariffs be charged on all products, including industrial products. The Community acceded to the first French demand. The negotiations which led to the Treaty of Rome had made it clear that the Community's agricultural market would be characterized by a high level of protectionism. This became even more apparent when the negotiated issues started to materialize. The French only had to compromise on the issue of industrial products, which led to a slight adjustment of the distorted relationship with Germany. The reasons for the success of the French policy have already been discussed. French participation was a necessary precondition, for which Germany was prepared to pay, and the German policy was not free of self-interest either. Besides the opportunity to rehabilitate, the country had gained an internal market which had given German industry full scope, even though the external opportunities were less than ideal due to the protectionist barriers. The relative agricultural balance of the other member states mirrored that of France, albeit in a less extreme form. The circumstances were particularly favourable for the Netherlands. However, in light of the country's transit function, the Dutch, like the Germans, were afraid that import duties would become too high.

Discrepancy between market and state

The European agricultural policy was successfully implemented towards the end of the 1960s. It developed in size and significance, and for many years it was the most important binding agent between member states, which had been prepared to integrate their national interests to form the European constellation described above. However, it would be fundamentally incorrect to describe their cooperation as a form of supranationalism. As mentioned earlier, the Community was in principle an intergovernmental system, although with relatively powerful institutions. The executive secretariat of the Community, the European Commission, was given an unprecedented range of authority. The Commission had the authority to formulate directives and regulations, which became the terms for resolutions passed by the Community. Another striking development was the establishment of the European Court of Justice. The member states were obliged to accept the rulings of the European Court and – partly as a result of the Court's ambitious interpretation of its duties – European jurisdiction gained force even without intra-state sanctions and direct parliamentary controls. Moreover, the Treaty of Rome not only provided for the removal of mutual trade barriers, it also instituted relief plans for 'weaker' regions and proposed campaigns to improve labour conditions and cultural exchange. And last but certainly not least, the Treaty laid the foundation for the agricultural policy discussed above.

Even though this system deviated from that of other international alliances, the Community became an intergovernmental rather than a supranational organization. This fact is borne out by the existence of the Council of Ministers, which consists of ministers from each of the member states, each of whom has to sanction a proposal before it becomes a resolution. This also applies to decisions on agricultural issues. Within this system, the movements of the Community are controlled, albeit indirectly, by the national governments and national parliaments of the member states. The compelling consequence of this system is that resolutions can only be passed if they are sanctioned unanimously by the Council of Ministers. As a result, the power of authority of national parliaments is (formally) not subject to delimitation and the sovereignty of the member states remains intact. This principle was later adjusted with the decision to institute systems of majority voting on all issues of lesser significance, provided that the member states unanimously sanctioned this form of decision making on a particular issue. Although the latter decision enhanced the decisiveness of the communal authorities, it was a questionable measure. It may be seen as a tentative step towards a supranational system, which did not reflect the true balance of authority. The power of the national parliaments would be curtailed without adequate compensation at the European level, which meant that resolutions passed by majority vote would lack the customary political sanction. These resolutions may therefore be seen as a contravention of the fundamental rights of member states. This 'democratic deficit' was compensated to a certain extent by increasing the powers of the European Parliament. This body originally only had an advisory voice and consisted of representatives sent by the national parliaments. Later the members of the Parliament were directly elected. It gained a veto on part of the budget prepared by the Commission and approved by the Council of Ministers. It did not, however, gain a general right to make amendments. Finally, a more recent development has been the acquisition of decision-making powers jointly with the Council of Ministers on, for example, the admission of new members and the conclusion of treaties with non-member states. Clearly the European Parliament has increased its powers. Nevertheless, it is not a parliament in the classical sense since it cannot originate legislation or pass legislation in its own right; the sovereign power still rests with the national states.

The Community's covert intergovernmental structure was both a strength and a weakness. Because the member states formally retained their sovereignty, the access threshold was low. However, the level of integration was therefore also low, which led to a number of problems. The aim of the Community had been to establish an internal free market, which presupposed two broad types of measures: those which removed the national barriers hampering free trade and competition, and those which were directed towards developing communal state control measures at a European level. In theory, these seem inextricably intertwined. Although opinions may differ concerning its exact nature, a common internal market presupposes some form of common state which is burdened with the control and protection of the internal market. However, although this interplay of factors may seem unavoidable to an outsider, the member states did not accept the consequences.

The first category of measures, the liberalization of the market, required the least effort, because member states did not have to relinquish or transfer their power of control but merely to limit or suspend control, whereby their sovereignty was not subject to direct delimitation. However, the same could not be said of the second category of measures, which would institute communal state control. Whereas the establishment of a communal market may be seen as 'negative integration', the establishment of a communal state may be seen as 'positive integration'. In the latter case the national power of control is not merely restricted, but is transferred to a supranational body.[6] It was at this juncture that the member states refused to go further. Consequently, there was a discrepancy between market and state formation from the outset. This divide was partially bridged when the member states agreed to negotiate the alignment of national controls and to standardize them to a certain extent. Agricultural policy is the most significant product of this alignment. Ten years later a number of the member states aligned their exchange rates in a similar manner, which led to the establishment of the European Monetary System in 1978. However, communal state control measures remained restricted, mainly because they were based on an intergovernmental system and the principle of unanimity, which implied that each member state had the power to veto any resolution. Some states hoped that the developing communal market would lead to a parallel development of a communal state by way of a series of *faits accomplis*. However, the opposite happened; the lack of communal state control measures hampered the liberalization of the market.

The discrepancy between negative and positive integration was mainly a product of the so-called European dilemma. The fear of national weakness prompted cooperation between the European states, but that same fear also held them back. The Treaty of Rome and its implementation may be seen as an effort to circumvent this dilemma, but in truth it only served to perpetuate it. The intractable nature of this dilemma is hardly surprising. In general, states try to avoid becoming absorbed into larger entities unless they are forced to do so. In the postwar arena, the United States and the threat from the Eastern Bloc had served as coercive factors which led to the establishment of NATO and later the Community. However, the United States did not use its influence to urge the Community to develop a supranational system with a state and market which were truly European because this would have weakened the Atlantic alliance which it dominated. Consequently, the Community was based on an intergovernmental system.

It should be remembered that the United States had little direct influence on the Treaty of Rome. It is possible that the Americans later regretted their detachment, particularly when it became apparent that the developing European market intended to keep the door to the world market firmly closed. Subsequently, the Americans instituted a counter-movement to bring the process back on to 'the right track'. However, their efforts were only partially successful. A number of tariffs were reduced during the 1960s as a result of the so-called Kennedy Round. These negotiations formed part of what is known as the GATT conference, where the interests of the European internal market repeatedly collided with the interests of the world market in general, and the American market in particular.

Delays

This tariff war was fought mainly in the agricultural sector, which was of vital importance for the founding and development of the Community. Once again the French led the attack and refused to budge, for economic and political reasons. Even though the European Defence Community had never materialized, the French, and particularly President De Gaulle, saw 'Europe' and the new alliance as a haven for French honour. The French therefore held aloof from the United States and Britain. Ten years after the European Community had been established, the British changed their minds and applied for membership, but the French rejected their application, arguing that they had been excluded from the American–British nuclear arms treaty. The French attitude irritated the other member states, particularly the Netherlands, which had developed enough self-confidence to openly contest the issue. However, the ensuing diplomatic skirmishes were as vague as the attitudes of both countries were ambivalent. Although the French thought 'European', their own interests came first. Thus they hoped to achieve what they called 'a Europe of the states', an alliance under French leadership involving economic and political cooperation by means of an intergovernmental system. The French were averse to far-reaching federal integration and refused to relinquish their sovereignty. The Netherlands realized what the French were striving for – which was fairly obvious – and undertook countermeasures by outdoing the French in 'Europeanism' and by plotting a course towards federalism. The Netherlands argued that federalism would enhance the democratic quality of the Community and would ensure that the smaller member states would not be dominated by the larger states. The first part of this rationale was accurate, at least in theory, but the second part was unsubstantiated, because it was contradictory and therefore questionable. Perhaps Dutch policy was not an objective in itself, but a tactical ploy to thwart the efforts of the French without seeming unfaithful to the European endeavour in general. Although it is unclear whether this ploy was intentional, it had an unmistakable effect. The Dutch proposal was doomed to fail, but this did not dampen the spirits of the Dutch government. More important was that French ambitions to transform the European Community had been thwarted and the balance between Continental and Atlantic relations, which was of importance to the Dutch, had been retained.[7]

In addition, the clash between the Dutch federalist and the French intergovernmental view caused the process of integration to stagnate, in spite of the fact that Britain, and later Ireland and Denmark, decided to join the Community after the French had diluted their ambitions. However, this extension of the community in 1973 did not accelerate the process of economic and political integration.

Nevertheless, the Community had materialized and although its progress was slow it had gained sufficient momentum to resist influence from outsiders, particularly the United States, which were experiencing a general slump in power at the time. Their humiliating defeat in South-east Asia in the early 1970s had given rise to the growing realization that they were incapable of maintaining the Imperium Americanum or, at least, that the costs of doing so were far in excess of the benefits. As a result, the Forum Americanum was also weakened, heralding the end of the Bretton Woods system and, consequently, the collapse of the dollar as the standard unit of currency. In the future, the dollar would also be subject to value fluctuations, which meant that the economic struggle would become even more unstable.

The fact that the United States was now less dominant in the global arena was emphasized by its position in relation to the Soviet Union. As in the West, the first three postwar decades had been a period of progress for Eastern Europe. The state-controlled economy had recuperated and productivity had increased, although it was still fairly low in comparison with the West.[8] As a result, the communist regime had been strengthened and was able to decrease the level of internal repression. The same applied to its external relations. By around 1960, it had become apparent that the state-controlled economy behind the iron curtain was capable of deploying a military force to equal that of the Americans. This was the start of an arms race, the more hard fought because it was between equals. However, the balance of destructive power also served to increase mutual trust, based on the belief that neither country would hazard a nuclear war or any other large-scale conventional attack. The anticipated self-control of the two superpowers locked them in a 'frozen clinch', and although this led to a rigid balance of global power it also brought stability and a measure of *détente*. This state of affairs apparently favoured the European Community. The United States had become less dominant, giving the European states more room to manoeuvre and thus allowing them to accelerate the process of integration. However, this was not the case. It is war, not peace, that forces states to forgo their independence and forge alliances. This applied equally to the Community. The new *détente* did not lessen the clash of interests on vital issues, and when tension mounted in the European arena the European states sought refuge as they always had: they turned to the United States for support, thereby ensuring the continued existence of their mutual dilemma.

SECOND PHASE: THE DILEMMA INTENSIFIES

Nevertheless, a breakthrough seemed to be close at hand. During the mid-1980s the European process of integration gained momentum. The driving force was an economic threat which loomed over the world market. Comparatively undisturbed competition had allowed the economies of the Pacific rim to grow to the detriment of those of the Atlantic. The consequences were far-reaching and began to manifest themselves around 1980. Private enterprise and governments witnessed falling revenues. Initially, it appeared as if the European states were going to implement the traditional solution which would result in a negative spiral of reciprocal taxation, similar to that which had led to the Great Depression. However, the danger was averted. The binding factors within the Forum Americanum proved stronger than the drive among the member states to protect their own interests. The Community was one of these binding factors, the member states deciding that they could not defeat an economic retreat by raising the external and internal walls of the European market.

However, the European states not only passively abandoned the traditional course of action but, more importantly, they undertook action. The economic threat which loomed outside their borders prompted the member states to make an unprecedented decision. This took the form of the Single European Act. The Act that was sanctioned by the member states of the Community in 1986 plotted a course towards a system characterized by the free exchange of people, goods, services and capital. Initially, the target date for the implementation of this system was 1992; this was later changed to 1993.[9]

The initiative for this surprising acceleration of the integration process – which was joined by Greece in 1981 and by Spain and Portugal in 1986 – was taken by a number of large European companies, including the Dutch company Philips.[10] Their main argument in support of integration was that European enterprise would lose out in the competitive world economy if internal markets were not freed of the multitude of duties and control measures, and if these were not integrated – as the European Community had promised – to form a single internal free market, similar to those in the United States and Japan. Philips' president, Dekker, had apparently donned the mantle of Adam Smith, who in the eighteenth century had argued that a large internal market was imperative for the prosperity of Britain. The appeal got a response, and although the member states of the Community were caught in a spiral of unavoidable cutbacks and other unfavourable circumstances, they bridged the internal divide and decided again to establish an internal free market.

The decision was remarkable, because the European states

seemed set to establish an internal free market without meeting the historical precondition of establishing a communal state. This unique endeavour to establish a 'stateless market' was pursued with verve, and it seemed that history, which usually taught lessons, was about to be taught a lesson itself.

The governments of the member states seemed resolute, but it was unclear whether they were aware of the unique nature and scope of their endeavour. Since the Community's foundation, markets and states had become ever more intricately entwined. This not only applied to actual tariffs, but also to taxation in general and to product and production standards as well as to social security programmes, environmental planning policies, industrial policies, police and justice departments and cultural affairs. In short, every conceivable organizational system featured an inextricable link between market and state; so much so in fact that the one could not be changed without directly or indirectly changing the other. National parliaments responsible for controlling these systems were apparently oblivious to the intricacy of the situation. The sanctioning of the Single European Act had been a symbolic act rather than a clear resolution, and the European states seemed unaware of the fact that the implementation of the Act not only implied that they would have to relinquish their own market but also that they would have to relinquish their own state. Although this ignorance may be blamed on a lack of insight into the matter, the taboo on the European dilemma was also an important factor. Integration had a 'nice' ring to it, but by openly addressing the sovereignty problem the governments risked the mobilization of public opposition, which would send the process of integration to an early grave. A 'code of silence' was therefore observed, in the hope that integration would be seen as a technical–organizational problem, enabling it to be realized without being hampered by nationalist sentiments. At the same time, it would gradually become apparent which state system was most suitable to control the market. Although the actions of insiders were questionable and undemocratic, they were understandable. Extending the negotiations to include problem of state as well as of market risked becoming bogged down in the age-old dilemma.

This more or less intentional ploy did not diminish the multitude of problems at hand. Would it be possible to establish an internal free market first and solve the problem of state later? The conditions seemed favourable. The economic crisis had been overcome with remarkable ease, even though the actual remedy, the European internal free market, had yet to be administered. Outside the Community the circumstances were rather more ambiguous. The disintegration of the Soviet Union increased the significance of integration and made the problems even more complex, for reasons discussed below. The role of reunited Germany was crucial. Which course would it take? Would the most powerful country in the European arena become a binding or a dividing factor? And what did the member states fear most: that Germany would go it alone or that it would increase its intra-European supremacy?

While developments in Eastern Europe forged ahead at an unprecedented rate, national and Community authorities worked on the implementation of the Single European Act. As the projected year of implementation approached, the public took a greater interest in the matter. Attention focused on the actual liberalization of the internal market and the parallel lifting of the internal control measures hampering free trade. However, what was more significant in this regard was the growing interest in the indirect consequences of economic integration. This interest was mainly directed towards national state control measures, which ensured equal competitive opportunities but seemed set to be curtailed without proportional compensation at the European level. This discrepancy between negative and positive integration, which had been a characteristic feature of the Community from the outset, had now reached a maximum in terms of the European dilemma. The discrepancy had not led to many manifest problems; the process of market liberalization – the negative integration – had been slow and therefore the gap with positive integration had hardly grown. However, the discrepancy now began to increase and, as a result, there was a so-called run-off of national controlling potential, which was not compensated for at a European level.

It seemed unavoidable that national parliaments would feel that they were being sidelined. However, this was not the case. No one sounded the alarm and none of the states threatened to put an end to liberalization if democratic control was not reinstated. This potentially volatile issue was covered up and Dutch members of parliament in particular started to set their sights on the European Parliament. They expected that the latter would be invested with normal parliamentary powers and so considered their own task completed. However, this was premature. The powers of the European Parliament to hold back legislation were increased, but none were instituted to initiate legislation.[11] Another area in which state controls diminished was in financial policy. Due to the coupling of currency values and the supremacy of the German Central Bank, policy margins at a national level had been grossly curtailed, without adequate compensation at a European level. The same applied to other government sectors, where national governments imposed limitations on policy. These sectors included the social security programme, the environment programme and national cultural policy. These limitations were not only imposed directly by the European Commission or the European Court but also indirectly, for fear of losing national competitive potential.

In short, the Single European Act revealed the true fields of tension and the painful dilemma confronting member states; their fear of national weakness had driven them to form a single market, but that same fear kept them from creating a state to control this market, the dramatic consequence being that sovereignty came under threat from the very forces striving to defend it.

Part II

NEGOTIATIONS

4

THREE SCENARIOS

The problems of 'state and market' were given increasing attention in the period following the conclusion of the Single European Act. Most of the publicity went to the so-called Treaty of Maastricht of 1992 which enshrined the principle of extensive monetary and political integration. Yet politicians and civil servants were also working in other ways, on the one hand to liberalize the market; on the other, to resolve the problem of state controls.

The question to be posed here is, which trend dominated in the negotiations and what effect did this have in general terms on the Community itself and on the individual member states? The three possible developments have already been outlined and are summarized here briefly.

THE DOWNWARD SPIRAL

The first possibility is the grimmest. It is based on the premise that the European dilemma will continue to exist and the gap between negative and positive integration will continue to widen. In this case a sombre future will witness national states limiting controls for fear of losing in the battle for competition and, because this is mutual, the downward spiral will continue unabated and as the market is made more open, controls will begin to disappear and civilization will come under threat. Sooner or later this downward movement will end economic liberalization, leading to a return to national boundaries and a resolution of the European dilemma by taking the road back.

TRANSFER OF SOVEREIGNTY

In contrast to this sombre prospect, there is a more positive scenario in which sovereignty is transferred to a European government and the gap between positive and negative integration is steadily diminished. In this case, depending on what is decided at supranational level, state functions which have developed the furthest are brought back into line. The fundamental difference with the first scenario however is that the 'free fall' of negative competition is avoided, although to what extent is not yet clear. The chance of achieving this variant is small, however. States are jealous of their sovereignty. Until now, states have only relinquished sovereignty if forced to do so, and it does not look like this will happen. Nevertheless, the threat of the first variant may encourage this trend and the resolution of the European dilemma along these lines.

INTERSTATE COOPERATION

The third and final scenario is the least dramatic. The 'free fall' is brought to a halt, not through the domination of some new supranational authority but through intergovernmental negotiations in a European Union context, effectively setting a limit to negative competition. This solution, in which the market is maintained and damage is limited without any formal transfer of sovereignty, is not dissimilar to previous attempts, even though these were not successful. Perhaps this is the way to stop the downward spiral, despite the fact that the level at which this is to be done and the extent of the agreements have yet to be determined. There is no higher authority here, and if each party has its own interests to protect, the problem may be solved on paper although in reality it will continue to exist.

It remains to be seen which of these three directions is the one towards which today's discussions are heading and what the consequences will be. Answers to these questions may be found in an examination of two examples of the problem of integration. The first concerns the open border policy and the Treaty of Schengen. The second is that of fraud and agricultural subsidies.

5

THE FIRST EXAMPLE: OPEN BORDERS AND THE TREATY OF SCHENGEN

FREE TRADE

A good example of the dangers that accompany liberalization of the market is the abandonment of border controls between the countries concerned.[1] The abandonment or relaxation of the work of frontier police and customs officials is a form of what we have described as negative integration. National decision-making powers are limited without this being compensated for at Community level with some form of positive integration. The potential result is that the national judicial system, a central pillar of the national civilizations, could come under threat and the level of civilization, particularly where this is relatively 'high', would find itself heading in a downward direction.[2]

An example of this problem is given in the French magazine *Libération* of 19 May 1989, in an interview with a person who was until recently a member of an international crime syndicate. He lived the 'good life' on the south coast of France and preferred to work in Northern Europe, where punishments are relatively light. He invested his profits in Spain where land is inexpensive. In fact, he bought an orangery there.

Although this is rather stereotypical, it nevertheless illustrates the point that integration has indeed freed the traffic of persons, goods and services while the curtailment and suspension of national regulations – in this case border controls – are not compensated for by action at a higher level. The consequence is that the potential for crime has increased.

In principle, this applies throughout the European Union. Criminals can step from one area of jurisdiction to another and so evade prosecution. If one also takes into account the fact that policies on

71

crime may vary from country to country the problem becomes even more complex. Compared to other non-European countries, the various judicial systems of countries within the European Union are largely similar. But differences do exist and these are central to the problem. They are most obvious in the level of restraint shown by the judiciary and in the scope of its powers – both having a direct influence on the potential increase in crime.[3]

As the example shows, a country where state laws are applied with restraint may attract crime from other countries, especially if border controls are relaxed. The same also applies in countries with extensive judicial controls. Countries where the judiciary has wide-ranging controls and extensive laws – which may not necessarily imply that more is prohibited in practice – may be equally subject to an increase in the crime rate. That is because, as the effectiveness of border controls is reduced, goods and persons otherwise subject to control are able to enter the country unnoticed. A third point concerns the fact that there is a relationship between restraint in enforcing controls and the scope of the judicial controls themselves. The potential for crime is greater where punishments are mild and where there is little that does not come within the scope of the law.

Fear of a downward spiral

The possible increase in the opportunities for crime, which is further evidenced by the rising number of reports concerning organized crime, leads in turn to the question of what will be the result of this increase.

There are three possible developments that connect with the three previous scenarios. In the first variant, which involves an absence of transferred national decision-making powers, the outlook seems sombre with national legal machineries becoming embroiled in negative competition. Countries afraid of attracting their neighbours' criminals feel bound either to increase punishments or to diminish the scope of their criminal law (*de jure* or *de facto*). In other words they are caught in a downward spiral in which the freedom of the market leads to serious challenges to the uniqueness and quality of the judicial system and therefore to a country's level of civilization.

Alternatively, there is a more positive scenario in which the transfer of sovereignty is agreed upon and where the gap between positive and negative integration narrows. Here too, depending upon the agreements at supranational level, national identities and institutions would still be affected. The fundamental difference with the first scenario however is that the free fall of negative competition is avoided, although to what extent is not yet clear.

The third and final scenario is rather less dramatic. The free fall is brought to a halt, not through an 'order' imposed by some new authority but through negotiations between states, whereby they effectively set a limit to negative competition through mutual trust. Here, too, the question is at which level will agreements be reached, and to what extent will they be honoured?

The Treaty of Schengen

On 14 June 1985, five member states of the European Community – France, Germany, Belgium, the Netherlands and Luxembourg – signed a treaty in the village of Schengen in Luxembourg. In this treaty they agreed to end mutual border restrictions and, as a compensatory measure, to introduce a number of other controls to be formulated in a supplementary treaty.

This treaty, known since as the Treaty of Schengen, formed part of the acceleration of European integration in the 1980s, and was to some extent brought about by Europe's weakening position in the world market. The more high-profile agreement of this period was the Single European Act, a supplement to the original Community treaty. It pointed the way towards a time when travel and transport of goods, services and capital would no longer be subject to restrictions.

As far as this is concerned the Treaty of Schengen is even more significant than the Single European Act. Apart from repealing certain existing national laws, it also sought to introduce new laws. The negotiations were difficult and only five Community members participated out of all the member countries, although a further three joined later. The relative differences between these five countries were smaller than those between the members of the Community as a whole, who were all originally supposed to participate.

In fact, these negotiations themselves and the proposed treaty can be seen as a model for agreements to be reached later in a Community context.

NEGOTIATIONS

The problem which the five countries faced may be simply described. How to reduce the potential for crime which open borders encourage?

All the participating countries agreed on what the problem was; however, because of the differences in their legal systems and national culture, the solutions proposed varied considerably.

Involvement

The first difference was the degree of involvement of the various countries at the negotiations.[4]

German eagerness

Of the five countries, Germany pushed hardest for the continuation of the negotiations. This typifies Germany's role in the European Union and reflects what has already been discussed in two ways. First, because of the lack of continuity of its state system, Germany has not placed its own sovereign interests ahead of those of other nations as much as the other countries have tended to do. This attitude is the result of internal tensions and of the tacit expectation of other countries that Germany should exercise restraint where this issue is concerned. They were and remain the nation that lost the war and a certain guilt-induced restraint is expected of them.

Incidentally, the location of Schengen is itself a good example of this restraint and the strong feelings it conceals. At first it appeared that the treaty would be signed in 1985 in Germany, because at that time this country was the host and chair of the negotiations. This was not to be the case. The other countries did not feel it was appropriate. Luxembourg was suggested as an alternative, since geographically it is the meeting point of all five countries. The treaty was finally signed in Schengen, without a word of protest from the Germans.

As we have seen, in economic terms, Germany is the strongest of the five nations. However, in the European league in terms of status it comes last, and this is very much to the advantage of the other countries. Germany is wealthy and cooperative and is the strongest force for European integration. However, this identification with the European cause is something of a problem. It is the result of a damaged national identity and as a consequence is at its strongest when chances of restoring its own unity are at their weakest. With the changes to this situation the perspective also changed. German identification with Europe has increasingly resembled that of other countries as Germany's national identification has grown.

Apart from the lack of continuity, there is a second point which explains Germany's strong sense of involvement, namely, the peculiarities of the German judicial system. With its hierarchic and legalistic constitution the German judicial apparatus deals with crime forcefully and consistently using wide-ranging controls. This means that Germany is vulnerable to crime which is dealt with less consistently in other countries and to activities that are not even defined as criminal in other countries. Thus Germany was particularly interested to see the negotiations succeed so that, together with its strong European identity and 'good' intentions, it appeared as if the German delegation would concede to any demands as long as they resulted in a workable compromise.

The Dutch merchant-preacher

As far as the degree of involvement is concerned, the Netherlands came a close second. The sanctions of the Dutch judicial system – in line with the country's egalitarianism – are restrained, although its laws – in line with the present centralized constitution – are far-reaching. As a result the increase in crime would be potentially dramatic; even more so indeed than in Germany. Thus the Netherlands had every reason to be involved. The Dutch press and parliament also played a part in stimulating Dutch involvement. While in the other countries the silence was deafening, in the Netherlands considerable attention was given to the negotiations. The tone, however, was mostly critical and gave vent to a typical Dutch fear that the negotiations threatened the tolerance of the Dutch judicial system.

These fears were typically nationalistic for another reason. Critics who advised that the proposed treaty should simply be scrapped failed to realize that without a treaty law and order would be just as much under threat from outside. This involvement of the press and the parliament proved to be a hindrance to the Dutch delegation. On the one hand, it did its best to keep the Dutch parliament informed; on the other, it upset the negotiation partners and as a result no one was satisfied.

The problems were obvious. Failure to close ranks in discussion was asking for trouble. First the negotiating position would be weakened since the opposition would be aware of the limitations; second, the negotiations themselves would be weakened because of pressure from the home front – having to withdraw from previously held positions and thus jeopardizing the trust of the negotiation partners.

Although the discussions in Schengen were quite amicable, the Dutch delegation was accused of dragging its feet because of the influence of the home front. This was justified to some extent because information concerning the Dutch position reached potential allies in other countries and put their delegations under pressure, too.

Finally, the image of the Dutch as negotiating partners was further weakened by what seemed to the other partners to be a certain ambiguity. According to them the Dutch delegation would often appear as upholders of the high moral ground, encouraged by their critical home front. This met with resistance. They may have been correct, morally speaking, but it was not always relevant, particularly when the point at issue was the ending of border controls. Resistance increased. As other delegates were heard to say, the 'preacher' would sometimes swap places with the 'merchant' with simple business interests hiding behind high morals. Dutch drug policies are a good example (see below). Initially, the Dutch defended their tolerant drug policy on humanitarian grounds. But when that argument was challenged it became clear that this policy was not only humanitarian, it was also inexpensive and posed no excessive burdens on the judicial system as in other countries. This change in argument seemed odd to the other delegations, but not to the Dutch themselves. They defended the second argument as they had defended the first, which the other delegations saw as pure obstinacy.

The other delegations saw the Dutch as 'merchant-preachers' because of the way they defended both their convictions out of self-interest and their interests from the standpoint of their convictions. This was not meant maliciously and even showed a certain respect; indeed it tended to encapsulate the Dutch character: an open market and tolerance with a national identity strong enough to defend both.

French reserve

The involvement of France and Belgium in the negotiations was relatively less than that of Germany and the Netherlands. This also reflected these countries' judicial systems which, compared with the Netherlands, operate repressively while being far less wide-ranging.

This French position changed, however, once the German and Dutch delegations got down to business and the French began to realize the importance of participating. At the same time a change occurred in the almost stereotypical view that the three other delegations had of the French. At first the French played a waiting game: reserved, slightly condescending and a touch arrogant. The French seemed willing to discuss anything, but appeared wounded if proposals were made that might involve changes to French law. This was never a serious obstacle and it tended to fade as the negotiations progressed. Nevertheless, the age-old tensions between the bourgeoisie and the aristocracy once more raised their ambivalent heads. The aristocrat was superior in status, even from the burgher's point of view, but when it comes to the exercise of real power times change. These tensions are still found in present-day relationships both between people as individuals and between national entities in Europe. Germany is the strongest country economically, but France remains on top in terms of status. This situation was reflected in the negotiations. While Germany charted out the territory France looked on and, as one of the other delegation members commented, only acted when it could do so with honour.

This view is of course something of a caricature. As the negotiations progressed the French played an increasingly important role. For example, one member of the French delegation went independently to Amsterdam in order to investigate Dutch drug policy.

However, this informal and individualistic approach was exceptional and contrasts with the strict formality of the French government hierarchy. One member of the Dutch delegation remarked that, if necessary, he could telephone senior officials and even the relevant minister at any time. In France this would be unthinkable. There, one would have to battle one's way up through the bureaucracy, not even to discuss matters with superiors but just to await orders. A good example of this procedure involves the French visa laws (see below). The traditional ties between France and its former colonies were cited as a reason for not extending visa regulations. The French position changed dramatically. Citizens of all countries, except those with Community or Swiss passports, would henceforth require a visa to enter France. This was decided from 'on high'. The reason appeared obvious; a wave of terrorism was dogging France at the time. However, the authoritarian way in which this was decreed surprised all the delegations, especially the Dutch. 'Order and obedience' as opposed to 'deliberation and mutual trust' dominated much as an aristocratic culture opposes the culture of 'merchants' and 'preachers'.

Belgian insecurity

The Belgians also apparently began without much enthusiasm. Unlike the French, the Belgian position was not seen as being one of 'superior reserve'. On the contrary, the country's delegation was noted for its cheerfulness. This Belgian, or more accurately Flemish, informality was not matched by the self-assurance that a prominent position in the Community would be expected to produce. In a sense, Belgium remained an outsider in the rivalries and negotiations of the other countries. The Belgians followed the progress of the negotiations but brought relatively little influence to bear. The reason for this is the relative weakness of the Belgian state apparatus. It was dominated from the early nineteenth century by the Walloon French-speaking aristocracy and, as a result, the state became the object of resistance when the Flemish, bourgeois population began to gain power.[5] After the Second World War mutual tensions mounted and central authority disintegrated into today's federal system. The judicial system has also been part of the problem. It is seen as relatively repressive, yet its range is limited and governed by particularist interests.

As far as the negotiations were concerned the Belgians recognized their administrative weakness. They noted, for example, that the four ministries responsible for the police failed to close ranks in the context of Schengen. It was certainly a pity, but unfortunately it was also reality. The divisive forces separating the Flemings and the Walloons proved greater than the forces of unity. Despite the obvious disadvantages at international level, the delegation members were themselves involved in these internal tensions and, when prompted, told anyone who asked all about the inequality in the balance of power at home and how little the other side could be trusted.

This national division was reflected at international level not only by their weak negotiating position but also by an increasing sense of isolation. Once again this was most apparent in the Flemings. When asked with which country they felt the most affinity, one Flemish delegate said,

> Well, not the Dutch, because they deserted us on the Flemish question and, as is often the case, the stronger of the two partners is unaware of the guilt which the weaker partner considers they should feel. As far as France is concerned, they have traditionally threatened and oppressed us, a role which the Germans have taken over this century. So, if there is one country we trust, it's Luxembourg.

The Belgian position led unavoidably to a feeling of inferiority, hidden behind a collective lust for the good life and a natural bonhomie. However, they made a virtue of necessity. For example, the Belgians were proud of their talent for improvisation. According to one member of the delegation, the Dutch seemed to prepare for each sitting as if it were a game of chess. 'Of course,' the delegate continued, 'in reality the moves were often different from those which they had anticipated.' With a certain mischievous pleasure he related how the Dutch had became rather confused, while the Belgians' improvisational talent had eventually triumphed.

Compulsory identification

National differences were also apparent, not just at the level of involvement in the discussions but also in the subjects that were discussed. A prime example is the question of identification.[6] Of the four countries, the Netherlands, like Britain, was the only country where citizens were not obliged by law to carry identification papers. In the other countries everyone had to be able to identify themselves at all times. In fact in Belgium the police have full powers to stop people simply to check if they have their identification papers with them and to make an arrest on the basis of this law.

These differences were interesting, as they were further confirmation of the relatively restrained judicial powers in the Netherlands where the state relies more on trust than on repressive measures. These differences were also significant because they shed light on the possible consequences of European integration, in terms of national characteristics. The relationship is obvious. In countries where identification was not required by law, the relaxation of border controls would result in a serious reduction in the regulatory capacity within that country. These countries would then perhaps find themselves having to comply with laws which were previously anathema to them.

This actually happened when the Dutch Minister of Justice proposed the introduction of compulsory identification passes. This proposal did not receive a warm welcome. It was seen as failing to recognize respect and trust and was a violation of the freedom of the individual. Moreover, it would lead to discrimination against ethnic minorities – which some initial research confirmed. Finally, it was argued that the measure would not be effective, and this too was confirmed by research.

These protests were effective in the short term and the Dutch Justice Minister dropped his proposals. Identification passes were not discussed any further in the context of Schengen. The resultant reduced chance of catching suspects was seen as a problem for the Dutch to solve alone. It was recognized that the chances of another country's authorities catching a suspect on Dutch soil were also diminished; however, the Dutch position was respected as being one of their typical peculiarities.

The other countries were very surprised however. For them, identification passes were not a controversial issue and the Dutch objections were seen as out of proportion and over-sensitive. In modern society, providing identification is so commonplace that it need no longer be seen as an official obligation. It is also a weapon in the fight against crime, and anyone who has ever been the victim of crime should regard carrying identification as a small but necessary inconvenience.

These arguments might well have convinced the Dutch populace but not, it seemed, its vocal press and parliament; at least, not at the time. Personal freedom and mutual trust were important principles and apparently the Dutch would rather be checked too little than too often by the police. As we have seen, the Dutch position was not challenged any further in Schengen. It remained to be seen however whether this 'civilized way of doing things' could survive in the long term. And indeed, the rejection of compulsory identification was only a postponement. The pressure of increasing incursion of crime from abroad led subsequently to legislation making it compulsory for people to be able to show proof of identify in particular circumstances, such as on public transport or at work. As far as the Dutch are concerned, in this respect the level of civilization has been lowered rather than raised.

Hunting weapons

Another illustration of national differences are the regulations relating to hunting weapons. In Germany and the Netherlands the possession of firearms is prohibited except for light hunting weapons, for which a licence is required. This corresponds to what was said earlier about the range of legal powers in these countries. In France, and to some extent in Belgium, the situation is different. In these countries light hunting weapons are freely available and a licence is only required for more powerful weapons.

The right to own a hunting weapon stems from the time of the Revolution. Before that it had been an aristocratic privilege to carry weapons. Curiously, with the abolition of aristocratic privilege the possession of hunting weapons was not outlawed for all citizens alike: rather the privilege of the few became, in however limited a form, a right for all. It is another illustration of how, even in its democratization, France has retained its grandeur. This residue is not an obscure relic of a bygone age. It is seen as a right that is jealously guarded, just as the freedom not to carry identification is in the Netherlands. Both are viewed as personal freedoms. However, the difference between the two examples is significant and, moreover, characteristic. The one is an active right which threatens others; the other is a passive right which in fact prevents a threat by others. It is a question of the difference in mutual accountability and identification, a difference that was reflected in the Schengen discussions.

As might have been expected, the Dutch and Germans faced a problem. Because what was forbidden in one place was allowed in another, they felt under threat and feared that the potential for crime would increase. Was there ever a chance that they would limit the range of their judicial systems and relax the laws relating to hunting weapons? Whatever the case, it was not to be. The Germans and the Dutch requested that the French and the Belgians widen the scope of their judicial controls. In spite of the potential controversy, the French and the Belgians agreed to introduce restrictions on the possession of hunting weapons. As a result, the range and powers of French and Belgian jurisdiction or legal systems were apparently effectively increased, and indeed in a very specific area revealed an 'upward' movement.

Drugs

A third and more controversial difference in national judicial systems concerns drug policies.[7] This is, in fact, a remarkable situation because in the last century a range of substances which are now called drugs were openly available. The trade and possession of these became subject to increasing prohibition during the twentieth century. In the 1960s there was an acceleration in this process through improved international facilities and a general trend towards experimentation. This occurred at a time when the supply of these drugs and the demand for them had increased considerably. The result was a flourishing of the drug culture which was subsequently chased underground as legal controls grew repressive. It was at this time that the fight against drugs became an international concern.

The Netherlands is an exception to the rule. Despite international treaties, sentences tended to be relatively light and prohibitions were related to the specific activities and drugs involved with a distinction being made between so-called hard and soft drugs. Physical addiction was an important consideration in the distinction and this led to a policy which, although not legalizing marijuana and hashish, does not penalize the small-scale use and trade of these drugs.

Drug policy is a good example of a distinguishing national characteristic. In contrast to what other countries might think, the Dutch government does not just simply allow its citizens to indulge in substances forbidden elsewhere! On the contrary, the Dutch judicial system is far-reaching and few areas of public life are not covered by regulatory controls. The crucial point is that, instead of heavy-handed law enforcement a considered and highly specific suspension of a legal provision may be made. Thus judicial controls are subject to highly controlled restraint.

As expected, the fight against drugs was placed high on the agenda in Schengen and all eyes were on the Dutch. They fought their corner well, and even though individuals may have had their doubts, they collectively defended Dutch national drug policy. Their first argument was a humanitarian one. In the Netherlands the prevailing attitude is not concentrated on punishing that which is against the law, but rather to heal and prevent. Drug addiction is seen as an illness. This policy has led to the free availability, on prescription, of the heroin alternative methadone, and even though 'patients' remain addicted they are brought into the orbit of the social and health care services. A similarly restrained policy operates with hashish and marijuana. Through official tolerance the use of these drugs has remained 'above ground' and this is believed to have reduced the likelihood of people resorting to the 'underground' hard drug culture. But, as before, the arguments of the Dutch preacher, or in this case doctor, failed to convince. The intention may have been laudable but the desired effect of decreased drug usage was difficult to prove.

The Dutch delegation modified its approach somewhat by pointing out that even though drug abuse remained a problem it was certainly no worse than in other countries. Its policy was also comparatively less expensive to follow than those of other countries. Although these arguments were good and should have improved the reception of the Dutch policy, this did not happen. The other delegations had such a deep and irrational distaste for drugs – in relation to the Dutch argument and also to the continued tolerance of legal drugs, such as alcohol, which also created its own share of problems – that the Dutch policy was seen, at best, as naive and, at worst, as cowardly. It seemed to the other delegates that they had been deserted by the Dutch in the fight against drugs and that the enemy could now infiltrate through the Netherlands as a base. It was highly exasperating that this betrayal was not admitted and that they hid behind a pretence that understanding was better than punishment, and cheaper too.

To the critics, the Dutch approach was not a realistic alternative. It was never really understood that this represented a closely considered flexible approach combined with restraint in the application of judicial controls, and not simply a desertion. The parties were therefore ranged on opposite sides, but because the Dutch had a vested interest in the progress of the talks they pledged to tighten their policy on drugs.

For an outsider, there were similarities between the drugs problem and the hunting weapons issue. In the latter case the French government had promised to extend its judicial control and in the former case the Dutch were to do the same. However, from the Dutch perspective the two situations were not in the least similar. A curtailment of the freedom to carry hunting weapons in France would require the extension of existing laws. This was not the case so far as drugs were concerned in the Netherlands. Although there are no prosecutions for the use of soft drugs, there are laws covering this area. So in this sense the French agreement required the extension of judicial control, while the Dutch concession required a limitation in the way the judicial apparatus is applied.

It proved impossible to bridge this cultural gap and the reason can be traced back to the variations in the power differentials of the countries concerned. In the Netherlands, power differentials such as those between young and old are relatively small, and intercommunication is not command-oriented – indeed it is seen by others as too liberal. Drug policy in the Netherlands is an essential part of the policy towards the younger generation and shares the very characteristics that so appal other countries. There, drugs offences are criminal offences and policy is seen as directed towards an external enemy to be dealt with a hard hand.

The Dutch concession was in itself modest, amounting to little more than a confirmation of other international agreements and certain restrictions on policies for the young. However, although these were quite minor they did represent an intrusion into the free social dialogue that exists there. Incidentally, it seems likely that similar changes in policy would have occurred even without the negotiations, due largely to the fact that the Dutch judicial system in general, and in particular as far as drugs are concerned, tends to attract crime from abroad.

The alternative scenario of the other countries adopting Dutch policies was unlikely. Although fear of the spread of Aids has put the subject into a new perspective. It is well known that in the Netherlands the distribution of clean needles has reduced the intravenous spread of the disease and this is because the problem is seen as being a medical rather than a criminal problem. However, the connection is hard to prove and up to the present day the official position in other countries has not changed. The authorities of large urban areas in north-west Germany, where the situation bears more similarities to that of the Netherlands than the rest of Germany, are the most sympathetic.

THE SOLUTIONS

What can be learned from the Schengen Supplementary Agreement which was signed in June 1990 but, despite subsequent ratification by the respective parliaments, was still waiting to be implemented in 1994? First of all, it was obvious that no country wanted their national judicial apparatus to move into free fall. Even though each country had its own interests, each had reason to fear that the potential for crime would increase. This brought the participants closer together.

This goodwill did not extend to the transference of powers of sovereignty. Their fears were not so great as to force them to agree to actual positive integration. In the transference of powers of sovereignty nations tend to be thrifty. The remaining option was the third possibility, that of multilateral cooperation, which was what Schengen was concerned with.

In broad terms, the agreements in the treaty were divided into two categories, the first being the specific promises of individual countries, which has already been dealt with, and the second concerning communal agreements.

Foreign police on home ground

The communal agreements in the proposed treaty fall into two categories: the first is concerned with the internal borders between the five countries and the second is concerned with the external borders of the five countries.

An example of the first is the mutual right, with certain exceptions, to continue a pursuit begun in one country across the border. While this would seem self-evident, one must imagine the scenario of a police car having to stop at the border while the suspect escapes to the other side. This subject proved to be controversial. The proposal was submitted by the German delegation, which is understandable if one considers the nature of the German judicial system. In the beginning, the French and Dutch delegations found it unacceptable. The very idea of German police officers operating on French or Dutch soil was an affront. This opinion changed, however. Once the aims of the discussions were considered the German proposal seemed more than reasonable. It was a necessary prerequisite to the 'open borders' policy and was eventually accepted by the other countries after various limitations had been decided upon.

This 'step forward' proves that negative integration, in this case the abolition of border controls, can lead to a form of cooperation whereby national pride and prejudice make way for common sense. There is, however, another side to the coin. This right of hot pursuit or *Nacheille*, as it is known in Germany, does involve one country's interference in the judicial monopoly of the other. Take, for example, a German police officer pursuing a suspect across the border for an offence which is against the law in Germany but not in the country to which the suspect has fled. This would be a clear infringement of judicial controls. If the second country is France and the pursuit involves the possession of a hunting weapon, actual control has been extended and its level increased. If, on the other hand, the second country were the Netherlands and the offence involved drugs, the result would be a reduction in the subtlety of Dutch drug policy and a reduction in the level of the judicial system.

It was only to be expected that those who followed this line of reasoning (especially the Dutch) would object to the right to 'transcendent' cross-border pursuit operations. This objection should, however, be put into perspective, because the German police already intended to pursue criminals across borders even if that right were not conceded, and in that case it would be without the guarantees formulated in the treaty. One of these guarantees was of major importance, namely, the principle of *ne bis in idem*, according to which a suspect may not be prosecuted more than once for the same offence. This rule as presented in the example had not been previously recognized by Germany, so that the state in fact retained the right to prosecute for offences which had already been dealt with by courts in another country. In the context of Schengen, Germany agreed to alter this policy, so that the *Nacheille* extension of the German judicial apparatus would be offset by the limitation of the principle of *ne bis in idem*.

Judicial cooperation

A second example of agreements relating to the open border policy concerns the different levels of judicial cooperation. The first involves the exchange of data; the second relates to extradition.

Both forms of legal cooperation have expanded considerably in recent decades with the result that legal authorities have acquired much more freedom to decide in which country a case is to be prosecuted. This development is increasingly distant from the nineteenth-century notion of territorial integrity which enshrined the principle that a crime should be prosecuted in the country in which it is committed. The abandonment of this principle is directly connected with the general expansion of international commerce and increased mobility which has resulted in growing numbers of crimes being committed in more than one country so that increasing numbers of criminals are pursued by more than one country. This development has been encouraged by the fast pace of European integration and especially by the open border policy.

As with cross-border pursuit, agreements in this area are intended to halt the increase in criminality and are based on common-sense measures. Nevertheless, it remains to be seen what the effects will be for national judicial monopolies. The basis in an assessment of this kind is the principle that each country aims to keep its own judicial system as intact as possible. If this is correct the conclusion must be that a country which attracts crime because its punishments are mild is forced to counteract by sending criminals from abroad back to their own country for trial. This protects the country's own judicial system by declaring that it does not apply to foreigners. In effect the adjustment is a downward adjustment. The effect would be a proportionate mirror image for a country in which the opposite happened: citizens of a country in which punishments were harsher would be sent back to their own country for trial. But this is not likely to happen. Even if the treaty were amended this kind of problem has not been sufficiently discussed. Germany, for example, would probably be unwilling to send Dutch citizens who bring small quantities of hashish into Germany back to the Netherlands for trial. In short, here too the conclusion must be that whatever the advantages of extending legal cooperation, the effect would be a downward movement, however small.

Controls on outer borders

The treaty also contains cooperative measures for controls on external borders. The first example presented here outlines the regulation of travel at airports according to the country of origin and destination. Highly significant in this regard, however, is the introduction of what has become known as the Schengen information system. This is a collection of data on wanted persons contributed by each country. As a proposal it was considered both logical and sensible. However, there are some less positive aspects. For example, a Dutchman might be stopped at the border between France and Spain because he is wanted by the German police.

The example illustrates how the disappearance of the common borders of the five countries actually reduces the likelihood of criminals being apprehended. However, this likelihood increases for criminals who venture outside their own countries. The consequences for national judicial monopolies are not that profound. It is true that officials in one country will be acting according to the rules of another, stopping people for offences which may be perfectly legal in their own country; but the implications are marginal and in fact all that is really happening is that the duties of the border police of one country have been taken over by those of another. Viewed in this light, the actual change is negligible.

Visa and asylum policies

The final example is perhaps also the most sensitive and concerns the admission of foreigners. This would not be a problem if all five countries were to have an identical visa and asylum policy; however, this is not the case.

There have been considerable changes in this area in recent years.[8] During the first decades after the Second World War the influx of foreigners did not cause many problems. In the main, immigrants came from former colonies or territories with other connections giving them free access to the motherland. They generally felt at home in the national culture and were usually able to support themselves, since there was a steady growth in employment. This scenario was also true for the people from the Mediterranean who migrated to Western Europe in the 1960s as guest workers. The cultural differences were generally greater, but as long as there was enough employment and the number of second generation guest workers remained small, the problems could be contained.

In the late 1970s the situation began to change. On the one hand unemployment started to rise; on the other, the influx of foreigners – especially from poor and troubled areas of Asia and Africa – began to increase. This twofold pressure resulted in a change of policy, first in the US and Canada and later in Western Europe. This change of attitude was also reflected in Schengen.

The change was most marked in France. When visa harmonization first came under discussion the French delegation began by stressing the warm bonds of friendship between France and its former colonies. Later on, with the rise of terrorism, France altered its policy and introduced visas for all other countries except Community and Swiss nationals. At the same time the German government was also preparing an extension of its visa laws, although less far-reaching. Moreover, just as in France, Germany began to implement a policy designed to discourage people from seeking asylum. This policy was also adopted by the Benelux countries, although Dutch asylum policy remained, together with that of Germany, the most friendly, or in any case the least unfriendly.

Despite overall agreement, there were many differences between the policies of the five countries and this led to problems. Here also the proposed treaty foresaw the five countries implementing each others' policies. In other words, a person travelling from outside the Schengen area to France and landing at Schiphol in the Netherlands would have their visa checked there. Thus far the situation is similar to that of the information system for border controls. However, problems arise if that same person has no visa for France, the ultimate destination, but does not need a visa in order to enter the Netherlands, which could happen. It would then be easy to travel from the Netherlands to France. As long as visa policies remain at odds, the proposed treaty will have little impact in this area.

The present situation appears to be disadvantageous to France, whose policy is frustrated, but advantageous to the Netherlands whose policy is maintained. However, this is not the case. The *route Hollandaise* tends to attract increasing numbers of people so that even without pressure from France there will have to be a negative adjustment to policy in the Netherlands.

Thus it is in the interest of the Netherlands, as well as that of France, to reach a decision on harmonization through negotiation. Policy will be adapted in a downward direction, although less drastically, for France may be prepared to make concessions.

There is a similar problem concerning asylum policy. The treaty contains various provisions, such as the agreement that only one country need handle the request for asylum. However, the question of who to allow in and who not to allow in has not been answered uniformly in the context of Schengen. As a result, the least unfriendly country naturally finds itself with the most problems. This applies to Germany and to a slightly lesser extent to the Netherlands, while the other countries, even where policy has been formally harmonized, are in practice more inclined to reject requests and are more repressive in the less 'humane' treatment of actually ignoring requests. Meanwhile, the effects of this policy discrepancy have forced certain amendments and it will be only a matter of time before we shall also see a clear downward trend in German and Dutch policies.

CONCLUSION: THE COMPETITION–MECHANISM AND THE HOSTAGE MODEL

Where national judicial controls are judged according to the criteria 'restraint' and 'scope', it would be generally true to say that of the four countries discussed here the level of the Dutch judicial system is 'higher' than that of the other countries, although the differences are relative and the Dutch application of controls with controlled restraint remains controversial in the eyes of the other countries.

Second, European integration – inasmuch as this is furthered by the Schengen proposals – has led in most cases to a slight 'downward' movement for those at the highest levels. This conclusion would at first seem to be somewhat negative, although the prospect is less sombre if one takes into account that the movement would be even stronger if there were no agreements in which compensatory 'upward' movements were agreed to by the other parties. Thus the treaty has all the hallmarks of reasonableness, and the negotiations were a success. Each side gave a little and took a little, so that no one country came out better than the others.

Yet this is not the whole picture. There has been no limitation of the sovereignty of the states concerned. The concessions have been 'adaptations', 'harmonizations' and 'support', but there is still no higher authority empowered by the five countries and capable of enforcing these measures. The treaty is based on self-interest and mutual trust. This is clear if one reviews the example of the open-ended visa policy. Because there was no higher power the negotiations were relatively relaxed, but at the same time the most sensitive problems remained unsolved or involved complex solutions.

In addition, even more significant was that no higher authority exists to hold countries to their promises, with the painful result that the actual implementation of the treaty is continually delayed. This is a good example of what is known as 'the paradox of collective action'.[9] The interests of parties involved are served by cooperating and there is a willingness to do so but, in the absence of a third party able to ensure that promises are kept, the cooperation never succeeds.

This theory is very black and white; it either succeeds or it does not. Reality is rather more subtle. The Treaty of Schengen shows that cooperation can be reached through interrelating various interests, both within the treaty and in the wider context of the

European Union. The higher authoritative power is in this case not a third party but a strong implicit expectation shared by all five countries. In other words, if one country breaks an agreement where its own interests are not involved, another country will do the same, thereby damaging the interests of the first country in another area. The countries are therefore each others' mutual hostages. This results from the extent to which interests are intertwined and of course to the actual realization of this fact.

Here we see the centripetal force which tends to bind countries that are already largely interdependent more closely together. The controls are not from a higher authority in this case. They are formed by mutually expected self-control based upon mutual trust and vulnerability.

This theory is similar to the idea of deterrence between two nuclear powers and may be offered as an alternative to the theory of competition–monopoly mechanism in which the paradox of collective action is solved by one country taking over another and extending its sovereignty.[10] The theory of mutual deterrence, the hostage theory, may be too optimistic and there is a risk, especially in the European Union – where the issues are less profound than in nuclear deterrence – that if one of the countries concerned reneges on an agreement the others could also lose their self-control. In this situation the centripetal forces of the hostage model would not be strong enough to break through the European dilemma. The lack of positive integration would result in increasing negative competition and would be difficult to stop. Even so, in the long term it should be possible to close the gap between negative and positive integration, but not by speeding up the positive but by slowing down the negative.

This solution to the dilemma, in which border controls would again be tightened, would be an all out attack on the very existence of the European Union.

6

THE SECOND EXAMPLE: AGRICULTURAL POLICY AND AGRICULTURAL FRAUD

FRAUD

The second example of tensions between market and state in the context of European integration is agricultural policy, and specifically the fraud associated with this. Although this is an old problem the relevant authorities only began to pay it special attention in the second half of the 1980s. One of these authorities was the European Court of Auditors, which in 1990 produced a report on the monitoring of the subsidized export of agricultural products. It begins as follows.[1]

One May morning in 1989, two controllers from the Court were in the port of Hamburg to check which inspection procedures were being applied to the transport of grain. The controllers were given to understand that the *Kapitan Danilkin*, a Russian ship which was docked alongside the port silos at the time of their visit, was being loaded with grain as part of a special community measure to dispose of a surplus of German wheat in other non-German markets. The controllers observed that grain was indeed being loaded at the ship's bow. They also noticed, however, that a similar transaction was being conducted at the ship's stern; on closer inspection the grain already in the ship appeared to be decreasing at a rapid rate rather than increasing. The grain was apparently being transferred through a port silo from the aft holds to the fore holds, a process which took several days to complete.[2]

The grain, so the report continues, was actually of French origin; it was being transported from Dunkirk to Russia. The intention of the transfer procedure in Hamburg was to acquire an official certificate of German origin for the cargo and thereby reap the subsidy which then applied to wheat of German origin. This manoeuvre, it later emerged, had become a regular practice involving Danish and British wheat as well. According to the European Court of Auditors, 40 million ecu of the total 57.5 million ecu cost of this subsidy was wrongfully paid out as a result of this technically legitimate irregularity.

This is a true story. A year later the trader whose grain was involved admitted that these kinds of practices were common. The rules allowed them and the state of competition forced traders to employ them.[3]

Many other examples can be cited in addition to this one of the grain circuit. On some occasions the European regulations are frankly violated, but often skilful use is also made of loopholes in the law. Imported raisins are offered for export as domestic produce, the same shipment of deep-frozen meat crosses the border more than once, pigs' trotters masquerade as steak, powdered milk for Africa is sold in the Middle East, the fat content of butter is lowered and then raised again, arrival documents are presented for goods that have never been shipped and so on.[4] The moral of all these reports is the same. The European agricultural policy is asking for fraud. The rules are too complicated, the subsidies too high and, in comparison, the monitoring procedures are found to be wanting. The sum expended in 1989 on these export subsidies amounted to approximately 10 billion ecu. If the experience with German grain were applied here, every year some 6 billion ecu could be disappearing into the wrong pockets. In the same year, 1989, a total of 26 billion ecu was paid in subsidies on agricultural products. Using the German grain example once again as a guideline, it could mean that 15 billion ecu was wrongfully allocated.

How is this happening? In its report the Court offers a number of explanations. It points to the discrepancy between the actual level of over-production and once presumed shortfall in European agricultural products, which still forms the basis for the subsidy regulation. Developing this argument, it reproaches the Commission for lacking good commercial sense when fixing subsidies, and therefore lacking a thrifty attitude towards Community funds. In addition, the European Court of Auditors points to the failure of the member states, who appear to have curtailed their monitoring procedures while actually receiving money from the Community to expand them.

These remarks are certainly valid, but avoid the issue of the

Community's *raison d'être* and therefore detract from the competency of the Court. Europe is a market without a state and therefore lacks the central power to compel its participants to accept a collective order.

INTERSTATE COMPETITION

Agricultural subsidies as binding agent

European agricultural policy offers one of the few examples in which liberalization of the market was accompanied at an early stage by the formation of state functions at the same level. These were the many forms of agricultural subsidy, which had been commonly employed at national level for some considerable time, and served to safeguard and protect the importance of individual countries' food supply. These functions were taken over by the Community from around 1970. The potential for negative interstate competition in the agricultural sphere was therefore prevented, albeit not by transfer of sovereignty (scenario 2), but by annual agreements regarding amounts in interstate negotiations (scenario 3) (see Chapter 4).[5]

This interstate control through subsidies on prices was confined to agriculture; however, it also enjoyed an importance that went beyond this market sector. For many years the subsidy system constituted the Community's most important binding agent. The development of this system reflects the nature of rivalries and cooperation between the founder members of the Community, in which France played a leading role. Indeed, French participation in the Community was essential, but its willingness to participate could not be taken for granted. On a previous occasion, with the European Defence Community at the beginning of the 1950s, France had drawn back at the interference in the national power of decision. And during discussions about an economic version of a possible European integration, it also hesitated after the military plan had failed.[6] This was to be expected. France feared losing the economic competitive struggle, particularly against Germany whose industrial products gave it a lead, and who might threaten French activity within a common market. However, it was chiefly in the agricultural sphere that France had major objections, being by far the largest agricultural producer among the potential participants and fearing that within a liberalized European market it would have to renounce its traditional protection of agricultural products. This determined France's conditions for entry. French agricultural policy had to be elevated to European policy, with duties on imports, subsidies on exports and a guaranteed sale at a guaranteed price for the remaining surpluses.

And this is what happened. The principal beneficiary was French agriculture which acquired a market that was fundamentally insatiable, offered a fixed price and could therefore be better described as an enormous storehouse rather than a market. Other countries also won this benefit, for example, the Netherlands for its dairy produce. The chief payer was Germany who in this way bought political respectability, acquired a European market for its industrial products, and moreover forced France to agree to shield the Community from the world market less drastically in this sphere than was traditional for this country.

The United States was an important onlooker in this exchange. Having made a decisive contribution to victory in the Second World War, the United States subsequently exerted great pressure on the national European economies to integrate. This was not an aim in itself, but part of this country's endeavour to create a 'free' world market under American protection. The French, however, tended to view this from a different perspective. France acquired in economic terms something which it had failed to gain in the political/military sphere: a Europe where French leadership had freed itself from American dominance and in which the participants were united, at least to some degree. This 'victory' was to be avidly grasped. In the years that followed, America's demands for tariffs to be lowered were met to a degree, but not on agricultural products. French interests were dominant in this area and they were defended with a passion which commanded the admiration of the other member states, but somehow resembled blackmail. This ambivalence towards the French attitude applied equally to the Community as a whole. French self-interest interfered at a more general level with the Community's relations with the United States, and in the wake of this with its relationship with Britain, whose entry into the community was blocked for several years. On the other hand, however, European agricultural protectionism meant that the Community soon became more than just an embryonic free trade zone. It developed into an interstate community of interests with centripetal institutions, which kept the fragile structure together whenever centrifugal tendencies threatened to gain ascendancy.

The agricultural bureaucracy in Brussels, which became strongly intertwined with the numerous national interest groups, gained the appearance of a supranational organization which imposed the income of the agricultural population from above. But that was not how it operated. Each year the national ministers of agriculture gathered to set the size of the subsidies. They only dispersed when all conflicts of interest had been forged into a compromise, like cardinals in conclave. These marathon sittings, as they were called, attracted public interest owing to the length of time they lasted. In fact, public surprise should have focused on another aspect. How was it possible for sovereign national states to reach agreement with each other year after year on the agricultural policy to be implemented, down to the smallest detail? We have seen the answer. Most of the countries benefited financially from the agricultural community and were therefore motivated by immediate self-interest, while only one country paid. This was Germany, a country which had for other reasons been reconciled with the course of events and accepted the disproportion between costs and benefits for what it was: a veiled and extended settlement of war debts which made possible the interstate protection of the Community market and prevented interstate competition in the agricultural sphere.

The control problem

It has already been noted that the intervention in the agricultural market was only one of the few examples of state controls on the embryonic European market. There was no control on other market sectors, or very little, while for one of the central state functions, judicial and police control, the national monopolies were upheld. This was also the case with control of Community agricultural policy, where several agreements were only reached at a rudimentary level.

The payment of subsidies and the decision to pay provide a salient example. Seen from a national state perspective, one would expect these two functions to be more or less managed by a single authority, but this was not how Community agricultural policy worked. Member states provided the Community with its own resources by surrendering 1 per cent of their value added tax (VAT) income and import duties on agricultural products. The subsidies were paid from these resources. The actual decision to pay, however, together with the procedure for checking the legitimacy of claims, became the province of the national states; by comparison, the authority of the Community's central instrument, the Commission, was slight. It was given the task of comparing national decisions with procedural law and transferring money from Brussels to a member state on this basis. In addition it was given the right to institute an *in situ* examination of the functioning of an organization handling subsidy payments, or another national organization entrusted with the monitoring of these payments, including customs. In reality, however, neither competency amounted to much because the former was only a formality and the latter was bound by the condition that the visit should be announced well in advance. As a result, the Commission's third 'weapon', refusal to reimburse, wholly or in part, subsidies which had already been granted, was not a serious deterrent owing to the lack of opportunity to gather convincing evidence. This 'sanction' lost even more force when it was decided that the Community would grant advances on the subsidies to the member states, the amount of which would be set by the states themselves. This meant that Brussels could only assess the legitimacy of the national payment in retrospect, with the result that the balance of control tipped even further to the advantage of Community components, at the expense of the Community as a whole.

This discrepancy between costs and benefits, and between payments and monitoring of payments, may be surprising, but it also reveals how each and every one of the member states were simply looking out for their own interests. This problem was not confined to agriculture. In a more general sphere the states were prepared to curtail their sovereignty with the formation of a common market, but they failed to transfer this sovereignty to a supranational body. The threat of negative competition was avoided for agriculture itself, thanks to German 'generosity', but not where the monitoring of this enormous industry was concerned. In the absence of a central authority, the member states' agricultural production and the subsidies on this production spiralled upward, while their national monitoring procedures spiralled downward.

The first movement can be regarded as a success (see Table 1). From the time of its construction, which took some ten years, the agricultural policy caused agrarian productivity to increase in all member states, transforming the Community from an importing market to an exporting market. In a certain sense this growth was intentional. The objective of the market and the pricing policy was to guarantee farmers a 'decent' income while at the same time increasing production strength. It succeeded. The prices that were

Table 1   Total spending by the Guarantee Department of the EAGGF
for various countries (in 1,000 million ecus)

Year	Belgium	Germany	France	Netherlands	Denmark	UK	Italy	Total
1971	0.1	0.4	0.7	0.3		0.4	2.0	
1972	0.1	0.5	1.0	0.3		0.6	2.5	
1973	0.2	0.6	1.0	0.5	0.3	0.2	0.6	3.6
1974	0.1	0.6	0.7	0.5	0.3	0.3	0.5	3.6
1975	0.2	0.6	1.2	0.5	0.3	0.8	0.9	4.7
1976	0.3	0.9	1.4	0.8	0.4	0.5	1.2	5.6
1977	0.4	1.2	1.6	0.9	0.6	0.4	1.0	6.6
1978	0.6	2.3	1.7	1.3	0.8	0.5	0.7	8.6
1979	0.8	2.3	2.3	1.4	0.6	0.9	1.6	10.4
1980	0.6	2.4	2.3	1.5	0.6	0.8	1.7	11.3
1981	0.5	2.0	3.1	1.1	0.5	1.0	2.0	10.9
1982	0.5	2.0	2.8	1.4	0.6	1.2	2.5	12.4
1983	0.6	2.8	3.4	1.5	0.7	1.4	2.8	15.8
1984	0.7	3.3	3.6	1.9	0.8	2.1	3.9	18.3
1985	0.8	3.5	4.6	2.0	0.8	1.9	3.4	19.7
1986	1.0	4.3	5.4	2.3	1.0	2.0	3.0	22.1
1987	0.7	3.8	5.6	2.6	1.0	2.0	4.0	22.9
1988	0.7	4.9	6.2	3.8	1.2	2.0	4.3	27.7
1989	0.6	4.2	5.0	3.8	1.0	1.8	4.7	26.0

Source: EAGGF Annual report – Brussels

set turned out to be so low that the sector was compelled to
introduce the usual efficiency measures, scaling up and mechaniza-
tion. These measures were implemented to such an extent that not
only did production per worker increase, but also per hectare and
per head of population – especially in France and the Netherlands.
What had not been anticipated, however, was the scale of this
increase and therefore the swing from shortfall to surplus. Such
success was too much of a good thing, for the producers as well. Even
though the agrarian sector could look forward to growing prosperity, realization dawned that this overproduction would lead
sooner or later to a reduction in production and therefore to
economic decline.

For the time being, however, such measures failed to materialize.

The policy had been constructed in such a way that in the short term the member states, and certainly their organized agriculture lobby, had an interest in pursuing it. Moreover, there was no central authority which might force them into change. So the upward pressure on production and therefore on subsidies continued. Meanwhile, in the countryside, and only publicized during the period of curiosity surrounding the annual marathon debates, the cows grazed and the farmers reaped; any produce not absorbed by the market went into storage at a guaranteed price. Subsidized export to the world market provided an alternative solution. This was in order to empty the infamous warehouses and cold stores packed with expensively bought, yet unsaleable produce. In fact this solution was illusory since actual costs did not fall. Moreover, it was simply a form of dumping which left traditional exporters such as the United States, Australia and New Zealand with a surplus of their own. The parties involved, however, regarded this export of the problematic surplus as a success. Negative publicity about unsaleable quantities of foodstuffs subsided, and the upward spiral of production and subsidies could once again continue uninterrupted, at least for the time being.

A similar silence surrounded the other problem, that of the national monitoring of subsidies and the accompanying danger posed by the downward spiral. The problem of monitoring, like that of overproduction, is now known to a wider circle. However, during the first fifteen years of the operational agricultural policy, from 1970 to 1985, only a small circle of interested parties was in on what can rightfully be described as a conspiracy; a conspiracy which brought the Community to life and kept it alive. These interested parties created both a negative competitive alliance and a negative community of interests, in which one party would leave another party alone, provided that they in turn would be left alone themselves. The consequences were not discussed. It was a taboo which served the interests of all the parties involved and, in a certain sense, even those of the Community, whose early existence would have been threatened by an open accusation. So the Commission kept silent when it should really have spoken out.

General trends

The annual reports on the funds from which the subsidy payments were made – the European Agriculture Guidance and Guarantee

Table 2   Estimated income transfers between EU member states as a result of agricultural policy in (1,000 million ecus)

Year	Germany	France	Italy	Netherlands	Britain	Denmark
1975	+30	+411	+203	−119	−188	−
1976	−196	+438	−1184	+146	−954	−23
1977	−992	+312	−185	+559	−316	+468
1978	−2621	−431	−2312	+310	−2064	+488
or						
1978	−837	+928	−1404	+1274	−1179	+794
1979	−1038	+1136	−999	+976	−1737	+956
1980	−1740	−36	−993	+1946	−1922	+1377

Source: G. Meester and D. Strijker, *Het Europese landbouwbeleid*, LEI/WRR, The Hague, 1985. Figures are taken from various research sources

Fund – offer silent witness. These reports reveal, in the first place, the success of the agricultural policy. Production increased, which meant subsidy expenditure also increased. In 1971, the first accounting year, the guarantee department paid out 2 billion ecu; in 1980, 11 billion, in 1986, 26 billion. As a percentage of the Community's gross internal product, subsidy expenditure for the same years rose from approximately 0.40 per cent to 0.55 per cent to about 0.70 per cent. Germany drew the shortest straw, while, according to the rather unreliable statistics, the other countries made a profit, with the exception of Italy and Britain (see Table 2).

The second point which emerges is the slowness of accounting procedures. The books show only closed years after the calendar year in question has passed; even then the figures do not always prove to be definitive or there are several circulating versions. This slowness and vagueness is understandable. The regulations are exceptionally complicated; moreover, the Commission lacks sanctions to compel the member states to act with greater speed. Its only recourse is a friendly request and the hope that, with the publicity surrounding the annual report, the accounting procedures will not become even slower.

This characterization is also true of the paragraph with which every report concludes; that which deals with irregularities. This begins unequivocally and states that monitoring the legitimacy of subsidy payments is essentially the responsibility of the member states. The message is clear. The Commission's authority in this

Table 3   Reported irregularities at the European Agricultural Guarantee Fund

Year	Belgium a	b	c	d	Germany a	b	c	d
1971	–	–	–	–	1.3	4	1	4
1972	–	–	–	–	5	0.3	5	0.3
1973	6	–	2	–	10	0.1	10	0.2
1974	–	–	–	–	21	0.2	18	0.2
1975	1	–	1	–	23	0.6	20	0.2
1976	3	–	2	–	28	0.7	24	0.3
1977	4	1.5	–	–	16	0.8	12	0.3
1978	–	–	–	–	16	0.3	13	0.3
1979	1	–	–	–	12	0.2	10	0.1
1980	4	4.8	2	0.0	17	2.4	12	0.3
1981	1	0.2	0.0	0.0	16	1.9	11	0.7
1982	1	0.2	0.0	0.0	21	1.5	12.4	0.2
1983	2	0.1	2	0.1	28	1.2	19	0.4
1984	2	0.0	2	0.0	15	0.7	9	0.1
1985	2	1.5	0.0	0.0	23	0.4	15	0.2
1986	6	6.0	1	0.0	24	0.2	14.4	0.1
1987	13	2.6	2	0.2	13	0.1	8.4	0.0
1988	4	0.1	1	0.0	9	8.2	5.4	0.1
1989	6	0.0	5	0.0	14.2	3.6	2.8	0.3
Average	4.4	0.9	0.8	0.0	13.6	1.3	9.5	0.3

Year	France a	b	c	d	Netherlands a	b	c	d
1971	–	–	–	–	1.6	–	1.6	–
1972	1	0.2	0.2	–	–	–	–	–
1973	1.4	0.2	0.8	0.1	0.4	–	0.4	–
1974	1	0.4	0.4	–	3	0.0	1.2	0.0
1975	1.5	0.0	0.6	0.0	2.8	–	2.8	–
1976	0.8	0.1	0.4	–	1.2	–	1.2	–
1977	1.6	0.2	0.4	–	3.6	0.4	2.8	–
1978	1.8	0.0	1.2	–	1.2	–	1.2	–
1979	6.4	0.0	4	0.0	2.4	0.0	2.4	0.0
1980	1.9	0.0	1.6	0.0	9	0.5	5	0.5
1981	3.6	0.0	2.1	0.0	3	0.0	3	0.0
1982	1.1	0.0	0.7	0.0	1.8	0.0	0.9	0.0
1983	0.4	0.0	0.1	0.0	1.5	0.6	0.9	0.6
1984	0.8	0.0	0.7	0.0	2	0.0	2	0.0
1985	4	0.1	4	0.0	1	0.0	1	0.0
1986	8	0.2	8	0.2	4	0.0	3.3	0.0
1987	11	0.5	9	0.2	27	0.1	25	0.1
1988	9	0.5	5.7	0.1	12	0.1	11	0.2
1989	17	0.9	10.4	0.4	22	3.8	14	0.4
Average	3.4	0.15	2.5	0.05	5.5	0.3	4.5	0.1

Year	Denmark				Britain			
	a	b	c	d	a	b	c	d
1971	–	–	–	–	–	–	–	–
1972	–	–	–	–	–	–	–	–
1973	0.6	–	0.6	–	0.5	–	0.5	–
1974	4.6	0.44	0.2	–	–	–	–	–
1975	17	0.3	17	0.3	2	0.1	–	–
1976	0.6	–	0.6	–	60	1	22	0.5
1977	9	0.3	8	0.1	28	0.6	2	0.2
1978	7	0.1	6	0.1	20	0.45	1	0.0
1979	7.3	–	2.6	–	13	0.2	0.5	–
1980	3.8	0.0	3.8	0.0	10	0.2	4.8	0.1
1981	10	0.1	7.7	0.0	8.8	0.2	5.2	0.1
1982	10	0.0	10	0.0	8.8	0.0	4	0.0
1983	14	0.0	14	0.0	2.4	0.0	0.4	0.0
1984	6	0.0	6	0.0	4.4	0.1	2.8	0.0
1985	13	0.3	13	0.3	6	0.3	3.6	0.2
1986	15	0.2	14	0.2	8.4	0.2	5.2	0.2
1987	9	0.1	9	0.1	37	0.5	26.4	0.1
1988	12	0.6	6	0.2	38	1.1	22.8	0.1
1989	20	10	7	1.5	64	1.8	43	0.3
Average	8.6	0.6	7.4	0.2	14	0.4	8.5	0.1

Year	Italy				Total EU[1]			
	a	b	c	d	a	b	c	d
1971	–	–	–	–	8	11.9	7	11.7
1972	–	–	–	–	20	2.3	16	1.0
1973	1	0.0	0.3	–	51	1.3	40	0.7
1974	2	–	0.6	–	89	4.4	71	1.0
1975	4	–	0.3	–	130	3.0	99	1.3
1976	0.6	–	–	–	226	5.3	127	2.3
1977	1.4	0.2	–	–	150	8.3	67	2.0
1978	0.3	–	–	–	113	2.1	61	1.0
1979	0.8	0.5	–	–	116	2.0	61	1.2
1980	4	0.0	3.4	0.0	182	19.0	123	4.0
1981	0.4	0.2	0.0	0.0	157	11.0	103	4.0
1982	6.8	5	0.4	0.2	192	33.0	95	2.0
1983	0.8	0.2	0.2	0.1	180	8.0	122	3.0
1984	3	0.8	6	0.1	127	8.0	79	1.0
1985	8	1.8	1	0.0	232	22.0	149	2.0
1986	10	3.8	0.6	0.0	313	30.0	195	4.0
1987	26	16.2	5	0.1	489	91.0	296	3.0
1988	16.2	20.6	3.8	0.4	367	155.0	201	3.0
1989	48.4	19.8	5.6	0.3	729	154.0	287	11.0
Average	7	3.7	1.0	0.0	204	29	116	3.1

Source: EOGFL annual reports – Brussels
Notes: The figures have been adjusted to accommodate national differences in

agricultural income taking Belgium as a basis. The figures quoted for this country are therefore real.

1   The total figures have not been adjusted and are therefore real.
a   Number of reported irregularities
b   Amount concerned under (a) in 1,000 million ecus
c   Number of completed claims
d   Amount concerned under (c) in 1,000 million ecus

respect is restricted, and so too is its culpability for what might happen. The actual tone of the report, however, is one of observation. Without recrimination or exoneration it repeats that the member states are not adhering to the agreements. They do not provide the Commission with the information it requires, or they provide too little, and they do not keep each other sufficiently informed of irregularities – the euphemistic term employed – which exceed national borders.

Indeed, the *pièce de résistance* of every annual report is the table showing the number of irregularities per country reported to the fund's guarantee department and what the countries had done with these irregularities. Thus each year four figures are assigned to each member state; the first of these figures indicates the number of irregularities reported, the second the sum involved, the third the number of reclaim settlements, and the fourth the sum which the member state has recovered and which would find its way back into the Community coffers from which it came (Table 3). The wealth of data collected provides an intriguing insight into what the negative community of interests was capable of in terms of subsidy control. An initial observation is that the level of irregularities, expressed in ecu and as a percentage of the total subsidy expenditure, did indeed increase over the years, but never amounted to more than 0.5 per cent, even at its highest point. In comparison with the otherwise scanty research into similar correspondences at national level, this figure is extremely low, which means it cannot be considered a reliable indicator.[7] This discrepancy points in the first place to insufficient reporting to Brussels by the member states. In the second place, more importantly, it indicates a low level of national monitoring in this area, revealing only a small percentage of the irregularities.

This initial conclusion, which confirms the results anticipated in scenario 1 (see Chapter 4), leads in turn to the following conclusion. Given that the 'dark number' of irregularities is presumably high, the differences over time and between the member states which the figures reveal do not relate to actual differences in the scale of criminality but to differences in the control implemented, the connection being the higher the figures, the higher the degree of control. Agricultural fraud is as widespread as fish in the sea, so that differences in the catch say more about the number of fishermen than they do about the stocks of fish. If this analogy is pursued, the following conclusions can be drawn. During the years 1971 to 1985 the figures for irregularities rose more or less equally with expenditure, although there were large fluctuations. This creates the impression that the monitoring as a whole maintained its – admittedly low – level but that, contrary to expectations, there could be no question of a negative development.

On closer inspection, however, the connections are different. The parallel development does not apply to all four figures but to only three. The number of irregularities reported, the sum involved and the number of sums reclaimed display a certain correlation which in turn correlates with the growth in expenditure. However, this connection does not apply to the fourth figure, the sum actually recovered; and this is crucial. As this sum is not only reclaimed but also has to be paid back by the member state, the figure may be deemed the best indicator for the level of national monitoring.

Of all the figures, this is the one which remains more or less constant over the years. It therefore fell in relation to the other figures which increased. The proper conclusion therefore reads that monitoring in the specified period of 1971 to 1985 did not remain at the same level but fell or was reduced, and that scenario 1's sombre expectation has to a certain degree been confirmed (see Chapter 4). The negative state competition led to a low degree of monitoring from the beginning and that level continued to fall. The compilers of the annual report themselves point out that the sums reclaimed lag behind the growth figures. However, from this observation they do not dare to draw the general conclusion that there was a downward spiral in monitoring. They simply report the 'facts' each year and keep silent about the system they are generating.

National differences

The positions which the member states concerned occupied in this process varied greatly. These different positions seem more to reflect the national monitoring apparatus in general than the differences in interest between these states in regard to agricultural subsidies.

Germany's position is striking. As has been shown, this country only had an indirect interest and so for this reason could feel it was the party least involved in the effective functioning of the subsidy system. The opposite is true. As has been previously remarked, this country has highly legalistic views on how a state should be organized. This requires the existence of a comprehensive and systematic apparatus of control in which in this particular context the customs department should be involved alongside the judicial and police organizations.

This national characteristic harks back to the creation of the German Empire in the last century. It is connected with the comparatively sharp contrasts in this country, whose inhabitants' mistrust of each other was offset by a communal belief in a legal structure which was not confined to their own state but was associated with universal pretensions. Following the Nazi dictatorship and its defeat in the Second World War, at a time when there was a great need to regain respectability, this belief in the actual function of the rule of law was once again reinforced, both nationally and internationally. One of the consequences has been that in Germany Community legislation has been systematically incorporated into its body of national legislation, while the other member states have limited themselves to introducing *ad hoc* adjustments.[8] This integration is not only theoretical but practical, as will be shown with regard to the subject under discussion, the monitoring of Community subsidies. Although Germany may have the least interest, at least where income from subsidies is concerned, it is the country where the European agreements are taken most seriously. Evidence of this is provided by the German figures for irregularities, which in the 1970s were certainly far higher than those of the other countries, and generally represented the majority of reported irregularities, both in terms of the number of cases and the money involved. Germany topped them all, being the best-behaved child in the class, even paying for the fun and always wanting to join in. This spirit is still widespread; but it is gradually decreasing as the declining figures show, particularly the drop in the sum actually reclaimed. The German law-abiding tendency has not been entirely able to withstand the temptation afforded by the behaviour of the other member states. This offers moderate confirmation of the expectation that, within this context of negative competition and cooperation, a country with a relatively high degree of controls will adjust itself 'down'.

In comparison with Germany, Italy and Belgium also occupy positions which are in keeping with their more general national characteristics. In both these countries the central authority is relatively weak and contrasts are significant between classes and especially regions. This is particularly true of Italy, which also contrasts with other member states of the Community in other respects. One example is the introduction of VAT, which led to major resistance in this country against the increasing powers of government. The same differences emerge in this connection. The slowness of communications from Rome to Brussels, about which the annual reports complain, particularly in the first years, provides another example, slightly off the subject but very revealing nevertheless. Moreover, Italy is reproached, in the form of an observation, for not paying out a major proportion of the financial advances provided by the Community, and for thus obtaining a rent-free loan on improper grounds.

Of greater interest, however, are the figures for the subject under discussion – the reported irregularities. Italy has a low score on all four fronts, particularly for the highly significant figure for sums which have actually been recovered. During the period in question nothing was recovered until 1982 and nothing paid back; the sums subsequently recovered and paid back were minor. As has been said, these figures do not indicate a low level of actual irregularities but a low level of monitoring, whose repressive powers are relatively harsh but whose scope and efficacy are relatively slight.

The same is true of Belgium, but to an even greater degree. Here the low figures also point to a low level of control on a general scale. These similarities are confirmed, not by Commission officials, but by representatives of international companies such as haulage firms. They describe Belgium as a southern European country located in the north, alluding here to such practices as the waiving of strict freight inspections in exchange for part of the freight.

Next in line is France. This country has a long-standing reputation for conducting strict customs inspections as part of its traditional protectionist and mercantilist policy; this dates back to the seventeenth century and is associated with the name of Colbert. The efficiency of its Community-related controls is not impressive. The French figures, particularly for the sum reclaimed, were higher than those of Belgium and Italy but lower than those of Germany.

The only area in which France outstripped its old rival is the percentage that the reclaimed amount forms of the total sum involved in irregularities. In France this was approximately 30 per cent and in Germany approximately 20 per cent. Both figures are low and refer to the general problem. However, the difference could also indicate that in legal-minded Germany the monitoring of subsidies is an end in itself, while in France more importance is attached to the anticipated feasibility of reclaiming wrongfully allotted sums. The French apparatus may be less bureaucratic than the German and therefore more bogged down by formality. However, what is important for the Community is that, despite the difference in percentages, the absolute figure which is reclaimed in Germany, adjusted to the scale of agricultural production, is almost ten times greater. It may therefore be concluded that, while the French approach may be effective on a national level, it is not in the Community's interests that this be the criterion. France also fails in comparison with Germany, and the suspicion is that while French controls may be strict, their approach may not provide the solution to the problem of particularist interests at European level.

The Netherlands, the last of the founder members, occupies a middle position. The percentage of the total sum that this country actually recovers is as high as in France, which means that there may also be a relatively high degree of efficiency. As for the total sum reclaimed the two countries vary. The Dutch sum is indeed lower than the German one but twice as high as the French figure, meaning that in the Netherlands relatively effective monitoring by the machinery of control is combined with what may be described as its relatively wide scope. In this instance too, such characteristics are in keeping with the nature of the central authority which has developed naturally and is therefore not repressive, and of the national contrasts within the Netherlands, which are comparatively minor.

This characterization of the Dutch control ratios is not self-evident to everyone, however. The remarkably large scale of agricultural production in this country and its prominent role in overseas exports and imports easily creates the impression that controls by customs and other authorities are somewhat casual. This problem will be further discussed shortly. In the meantime, suffice it to say that this suspicion appears not to be supported by the figures, at least not the usual interpretation generally associated with these figures.

Finally, the two later additions to the Community, Denmark and Britain, are discussed. The former occupies a position between Germany and the Netherlands, thereby confirming the connection made between a stable central authority and comparatively minor internal tensions on the one hand, and a high level of control on the other. Britain's position is more complicated. The number of reported irregularities is high, at least in the early period, and approaches the German level, which could indicate that the control is similarly thorough. On closer inspection, however, this view is incorrect. Contrary to the situation in Germany, the reported irregularities are concentrated in a specific region, Northern Ireland. Here, the central authority is contested, so the tendency for irregularities to occur is relatively high until 'hard' measures are taken. These figures contrast with those for the British mainland. The number of reported irregularities – adjusted for the Northern Ireland problem – and the sums involved, whether claimed back or not, resemble those of Denmark and especially those of the Netherlands. This similarity is clear. All three countries have, in their own fashion, a strong, natural central authority and, in comparison with the other member states, minor social contrasts, although of the three countries Britain has the most. This country's similarity with the Netherlands is also augmented by its free trade history which has resulted in the creation of a machinery of government which traditionally remains reserved and is not very repressive in monitoring the import and export of goods, and by extension the traffic of people and ideas. A major difference, however, is that in Britain trade liberalism is much more strongly associated with a high degree of nationalism than it is in the Netherlands. This greatly impedes the process of economic and political integration, as is discussed below.

INTERSTATE NEGOTIATIONS

The relative positions of the Community member states underwent a clear and sudden change towards the end of the period under consideration. The reported irregularities from 1985 have begun to rise, outstripping the increase in total fund expenditure.

What is remarkable is that this movement only occurs at one end of the spectrum. Where the degree of control is relatively low, as argued here, the level increases. This is evident most strongly in Italy, but also applies to Belgium and France. Moreover, the rise is seen in all four figures, and therefore also in the most important of these, which reflects the sums claimed back.

At the other end of the scale from this upward movement, however, is a downward movement in the country with the highest levels, Germany. The figures for the remaining countries stay more or less the same. The net result of this adjustment at both ends is modest. The number of reported irregularities grows considerably, but the total sum claimed back is much less. Nevertheless, the change of course is clear and the question arises: how has the spell of negative competition and cooperation been broken?

The change of course

This adjustment in control ratios provided by the figures does indeed express what may be described as a breakthrough in the taboo. The conspiracy of silence surrounding agricultural subsidies, which had constituted a significant but secret binding agent, and the inadequate controls on subsidies, made way for public indignation.

The decisive factor which provoked this change was not the guilty conscience of the parties immediately involved but simple external pressure. The Community's income was stagnating. Agricultural subsidy payments were a great strain on the Community's budget; they were growing both in absolute and relative terms, and therefore represented an increasing threat to other expenditure and related interests. However, as long as economic growth continued and central sources of income rose, this tension would not lead to disputes endangering the system as such. This was also the case with similar problems within the member countries. The situation changed, however, towards the end of the 1970s when shifts in the world market became evident, and therefore in the global balance of power which had developed after the war. In Europe and the Atlantic-oriented region of the United States, economic growth stagnated. The consequences are well known: there was a steep rise in unemployment, particularly when governments also saw their income fall and adjusted their policies accordingly.

The Community followed the trend. Its income was directly related to that of its member states; not being a sovereign power like these countries and therefore lacking the capacity to create a budget deficit, the Community found itself compelled to control the ever-growing agricultural expenditure. This brought agricultural policy, and therefore the monitoring problem, into the open for the first time. Parties who had little or no interest in the dominant clique saw their chance and made use of the public sense of justice to get the ratios adjusted in their favour.

Who were these relative outsiders? As is often the case it was a meeting of the two extremes. At the one extreme there was the Dutch member of the European Parliament, Piet Dankert, who raised the question of fraud. His chief aim was to generally strengthen the control and therefore the power of the central body – the Commission – and by extension his own European Parliament. He opted for scenario 2: the stopping of interstate competition through formal transfer of sovereignty to Brussels.[9]

At the other extreme stood Britain in the person of its prime minister, Margaret Thatcher.[10] The ambivalent attitude to European integration present in all member states was most strongly felt and plainly expressed in this country. Thatcher was an eloquent exponent of this view. She personified the neo-liberalism, mixed with strong conservative and nationalistic elements, which had gained in strength as a result of the economic recession in the countries of Western Europe. This was particularly the case in Britain where the problems had manifested themselves at an early stage and moreover contrasted with the country's not so distant glorious past. The position taken by the then prime minister was clear, at least at first sight, and was in keeping with her political ideology. The Community was an embryonic free market which in her opinion required no state controls, at any rate less than at the level aspired to by Brussels bureaucrats. There was no transfer of sovereign rights in her vision of the Community. It offended her nationalism and would only frustrate the free market mechanism. Her ideal appeared to be a market without statehood, regarded as anathema by others. So the British Prime Minister aimed her arrows at the Community fraud in a deliberate attempt, as British officials later described it, to discredit the 'hated' Brussels bureaucracy while protecting British sovereignty and the free market. In so doing, Britain in fact opted for the hideous scenario 2, in which states who form a free market become engaged in a negative competition struggle through which they threaten their own identity. The British Prime Minister was apparently unperturbed by this danger, which also threatened Britain. It may be that belief in a free market and nationalism prevented her from seeing that these two principles were mutually incompatible. Be that as it may, this attack certainly woke up some sleeping dogs. The consequences, however, were not what she had intended. The charge of fraud exposed the lack of monitoring and led to more, not less, intervention by the Commission and its bureaucrats.

This movement did not gain ground to such an extent that Thatcher's opponents triumphed and the member states transferred sovereignty in accordance with scenario 2. The actual developments followed scenario 3: it was attempted, through interstate negotiations with the Commission as a mediating third party, to neutralize the negative competition and adjust the monitoring level upward.

These dealings provide a complicated picture of twelve member states who on the one hand form a united front towards the Commission and the outside world, while on the other hand, as competitors, they watch each other with suspicion. Their relationship was marked by this double strategy from the very beginning, but the pressure of cutbacks and public opinion shifted the balance from negative cooperation to mutual rivalry. The united front began to split, exposing member states' differences which were to intensify the picture already presented.

Southern Europe

The first victim to fall was Italy. The situation which had been observed in the annual report figures was confirmed by specific research. Subsidy monitoring in this country was found to be seriously unreliable. It is true that sanctions were comparatively severe, and that checks, if these were carried out at all, were precise and physical. For this reason, however, they lacked the scope of a document check, which was generally conducted retrospectively, but was more 'risk rational' and therefore less susceptible to corruption. Italian subsidy monitoring which, as has already been mentioned, was in keeping with the general situation of a weak central authority and comparatively marked social differences, was regarded as primitive by the representatives of the northern countries whose monitoring was more administrative in nature. Unmistakable feelings of superiority and inferiority were bound up in these differences. Such feelings had previously been concealed out of courtesy which had been reinforced by the common interest. Now the Commission saw its chance and implemented measures for which it had received a mandate from the member states. It operated with caution. Although the Commission did possess the formal right to hold back payments to member states, this sanction was expected to produce a negative effect. It was feared that member states would reduce their cooperation to a minimum which, given the Commission's lack of authority to implement its own investigations, would make the task of proving fraud extremely difficult, if not impossible. Moreover, it was most unlikely that they would adopt a more cooperative attitude in the future. It has already been stated that the Commission's position was that of a mediator rather than that of a central authority. It therefore sought its strength not in sanctions but in using the positive incentives of financial and technical support to strengthen the machinery of control in collaboration with the local and national authorities. This tactic enjoyed some success. Italian officials were provided with modern facilities; for example, an automated databank with information on sectors such as the number of registered olive trees and the amount of olive oil obtained from these trees. Moreover, they were given a helicopter to compare data on the screen with observation from the air. The effects of this policy, which was implemented in about 1986, was reflected in the annual report figures for Italy; these shot up during this period. Thus it apparently improved, and the same methods would be applied a little later in the other southern European member states of the Community who had entered the Union at a later date and faced similar problems to an even greater degree. The effects of the policy in these countries are quite evident. Although there will continue to be differences for some considerable time, the monitoring level in the southern countries is nevertheless being adjusted upward, and the spell of negative competition seems to be being broken to some extent.

Northern Europe

Following this relative success on the southern front it was the turn of Northern Europe. In the meantime, the fraud problem had acquired greater importance and a separate unit had been established within the Brussels bureaucracy whose purpose was to coordinate the battle against fraud. With the setting up of this unit the Commission had gathered enough strength and courage to subject subsidy monitoring procedures in the other countries to closer scrutiny as well. Similar methods were employed; the emphasis lay on cooperation, coordination and harmonization; the underlying threat of a fine, although mentioned on several occasions, was not implemented even within this new relationship. The Commission was supported by the European Court, which was prompted by a fraud case involving high officials of the Greek government to once again stress that the member states should regard it as their duty to handle Community finances in the same manner as national funds, and therefore provide equal forms of control, both administrative and judicial. A similar role was played by the European Court of Auditors which in its own way had actually identified the lack of monitoring. One of the targets for condemnation was the Commission itself which had been satisfied with too little too soon; it was censured by the Court in its 1990 report for lacking market insight and for an uneconomical approach when fixing subsidies. The member states, however, were responsible for the actual control procedures, and were most at fault in this area. The Court report had initially been obstructed because of its frank approach. This was common practice within the culture of negative competition and negative cooperation in which this Community institution had also participated. Now that the taboo had been broken the report was published; although it provoked some outmoded censure, it strengthened the Commission's position. This weakened the member states' position, as their reactions to the Commission's new zeal show. At first, their attitude to the regular requests from Brussels for more data and greater cooperation was polite but laconic. The national customs authorities or other monitoring organizations began to be alarmed when the Community accountants announced that they would visit. The major reason for this alarm was the aggressive character which these inspections had acquired since the period between announcing the visit and its actual occurrence had been drastically reduced, and the threat of fines had been intensified. All these factors greatly increased member states' inclination to cooperate with each other. A first, fairly faultless example is provided by an exchange programme between the various national customs organizations which for a considerable time now has allowed Greek or Italian customs officials to work with Dutch or German colleagues and vice versa. Although the task of mutual inspection is not an official objective, as it was for the German Zollverein, in practice this collaboration does tend to increase control. Another example is provided by the exchange of information on the formal structure of control procedures, their practical application and the irregularities identified. Such an exchange had previously been mired in good intentions; now an official databank was instituted to which all the member states were connected. A third and final example is provided by the actual monitoring procedures. It was unanimously resolved to introduce as of 1 July 1992 the now infamous norm of a minimum 5 per cent physical inspection of exports of agricultural produce eligible for subsidy. As will be shown later, this resolution in particular constituted a violation of national autonomy which would present the member states concerned with major problems.

At first, however, the new cooperation proceeded without much opposition. Moreover, now that the member states have acquired their first experience of the system, their national representatives generally endorse the new direction. Questions about tensions and rivalry are disregarded as hardly relevant. The problems are considered technical, with the negotiations being conducted by specialists far removed from the spheres of politics and publicity, which prevailing opinion considers is probably for the best.

This consensus, however, is largely superficial. While the technical argument is relevant – the monitoring problems are complicated and constitute a separate issue – it is used to keep the reins in the hands of specific organizations. This is particularly the case with the Commission, whose members know from experience that if the Community's problems come to be expressed in terms of interstate competitive relationships, its role as an intermediary will be marginalized and national politicians will take centre stage. The same is also true of national specialists whose first loyalty is to their own office or department; the interests of such bodies may not always be served when problems are dealt with at a higher level.

The technical veil drawn across the real issues is in fact somewhat transparent. All the relevant parties recognize that they are entangled in problems which are too extensive to deal with. The observations made in the European Court of Auditors' report are the simple truth. The subsidy monitoring procedures are insufficient. There is a tradition of this, with the emphasis on imported products which brought in revenue; there was also the threat of some kind of contagion from abroad. In the case of exports the situation was reversed. Subsidies were non-existent or insignificant; responsibility for checking that the exported goods met requirements was principally the concern of the country importing them.

This situation changed with the advent of the European Union; what changed little, if at all, were the monitoring procedures. These lagged behind, for reasons which have already been explained. None of the parties concerned has in fact a clear insight into their own shortcomings. That the system does not function is certain, and because it does not function the major faults cannot be identified. It is significant to note that not one of the countries compiles its own national statistics on the scale and nature of agricultural fraud. The problem appears to vanish in the bureaucracy of the general detection and prosecution work conducted by the relevant organizations with the experts finding it difficult to gain access to even general data. It is even more difficult for the interested outsider – access is simply denied to anyone managing to find a way through the labyrinths of the relevant departments. This denial of access is also typical of the judicial authorities, particularly the prosecutors. Their control function has also recently been revitalized. For some time now lawyers from the member states have been conferring with each other; like customs officers they exchange experiences, explore the many gaps between the national judicial systems and, if possible, close them. The limited amount of access allowed to third parties is surprising. Prosecution of subsidy cases is extremely complex, requiring knowledge with which only specialists are familiar; moreover, all kinds of local, national and international interests are tied up in such cases. The most significant factor, here and with other agencies, however, is that, judged by its own standards, control procedures are insufficient. The result is that the researcher is little more than a frustrated snooper.

National differences

Alongside these similarities between the Northern Europe member states there are remarkable differences which are of interest, as they are directly connected to the economic competition that tends not to be mentioned so often.

The Netherlands

The Netherlands occupies a special place in this area of tension between the Northern Europe member states of the Community. It is one of the smallest members of the Community geographically, but its port, Rotterdam, is the largest in the world, and by far the largest in the European Union. In addition, most of the subsidized agricultural produce is exported via Rotterdam. The monitoring procedures applied to this gigantic flow of goods have been adapted accordingly and are the opposite of those employed in the southern countries. Dutch procedures are heavily weighted towards examination of commercial documentation, with relatively few time-consuming physical checks. Moreover, the system is not very repressive. Official sanctions are lenient and are avoided wherever possible by settlement at an early stage of control, leading to a situation where relations between government and business are based less on command and obedience and more on consultation and mutual trust than in other countries. An example of this is provided by what is known as the Femac (the Dutch abbreviation for fictitious entrepôt with administrative control) rule; a company may be granted a licence for a specified period to conduct its own administrative controls, on condition that its administration will remain open for retrospective inspection. Clearly, such an arrangement is of interest to both parties, for it increases the rate of goods' flow and eases the workload for customs.

This typical example of Dutch flexibility supports what has been previously said about this country. Relations are comparatively egalitarian, and the government is a self-evident and barely contested central authority which, in accordance with general domestic relations, rarely exercises direct power but uses this to bring various parties to reach a compromise through consultation. This characteristic can be traced back earlier to when the Netherlands was still a strongly federalist republic, and the middle-class merchant elite – and through them large sections of the population – had a vested interest in maintaining a government whose rule was tolerant. This interest was of long duration and found expression in the law which – as has previously been remarked – is unique to this country in prescribing that government control should impede free trade as little as possible.

This same flexibility is also a feature of monitoring procedures for the export of agricultural produce, together with the payment of subsidies on such produce. Typically for the Netherlands, these subsidies are not paid out by the government itself but by agricultural boards in which government and business combine forces. Both procedures – monitoring and payment – are administratively connected, as they are in other countries, but the nature of the Dutch system is that it maintains the least number of procedures and that exporters receive payment more quickly here than anywhere else.

Understandably, this Dutch facility provokes responses from the other countries, allies and competitors. It is most significant that experts from these other countries individually express their admiration for the Dutch approach which they describe as advanced. Although it is worthy of emulation there are various difficulties. For example, in France the business community is strongly in favour of adapting to the Dutch model, but the government is hesitant and the unions remain adamantly opposed to such a move. They fear – and with justification – that adoption of the Dutch method would lead to a reduction in the physical controls by less skilled workers, and would thus result in unemployment.

Naturally, however, the Dutch system is criticized as well as admired. Although it is seen to be flexible, it is also alleged that it is *too* convenient, *too* friendly or downright lax. Sometimes such criticism is openly expressed. The port of Rotterdam has been accused of unfair competition by enticing the business community in one promotional brochure with the promise of absolutely no physical checks on goods. Furthermore, according to another accusation, cooperation between the government and the business community has led to official statistics on agricultural production being systematically adjusted upward, thereby increasing the Dutch share of subsidies. The accusation of unfair competition is heard in most conversations criticizing the Dutch system. French representatives are the most openly critical; they clearly regret that trade has moved away from ports such as Le Havre in favour of Rotterdam. A similar situation is more or less true of Belgium and the port of Antwerp where there is also a certain *jalousie de métier* which is reinforced by what must be described as a lack of cultural understanding. The control relations in both France and Belgium are more southern and therefore much more repressive, based on mistrust rather than good faith. For this reason representatives of these countries suspect that Dutch procedures would generate a form of abuse if imported, although such abuse may not necessarily exist in the Netherlands.

Dutch representatives dismiss these criticisms. The example of the propaganda circulated about Rotterdam is refuted by the observation that inspections of documents are superior to physical inspections. They in fact regard their own approach as more advanced and appear somewhat aggrieved by the accusation. This is a general reaction. Representatives of the Dutch Ministry of Agriculture dismiss the accusation of statistical manipulation by the agriculture boards and refer accusers to Eurostat, the Community's statistical bureau, which would have articulated such criticism had there been any foundation for it. The officials sigh and declare that they stand alone where defence of the Dutch method is concerned. Criticism such as this is understandable. The high productivity of Dutch agriculture in general inspires envy which is reinforced by the speed with which controls are conducted. However, the criticism itself is described as unjust. In Community discussions the Netherlands often advocates greater control, particularly of regulations which are open to better control. An example of this situation is the raisin problem. In order to promote Greek interests, a relatively high guarantee price was set for raisins. An unintentional result of this, however, was that many Turkish raisins were offered for export as Greek raisins. This also affected Rotterdam where Dutch controllers tackled the problem. However, their initiative was not adopted by the other countries, with the result that mainly smaller, local traders were caught and saw their businesses fail, while the larger concerns moved away and continued their practices in other locations. 'Nobody was bothered,' declare the Dutch representatives. 'Our zeal was even turned against us in half-veiled insinuations that the problem was confined to the Netherlands and that was why we were so concerned by it. Only Greece supported us, but it's better not to have the support of a southern country!'

An example with similar scope is the fish scandal. As is well known, the Dutch fishing fleet's capacity conflicts with the allocated quota, so more fish are caught than permitted. This problem was openly debated in the Dutch parliament, the Dutch attitude being that this is a simple question of people being obliged to keep to the rules. In other countries, however, there is a suspicion that anyone who washes their dirty linen in public must have a great deal more to hide.

This cultural misunderstanding between the two sides continues when control becomes judicial in nature and these differences emerge. A crucial element in this is the public prosecution service's comparatively autonomous position in relation to the legal system and its own government. This position causes international confusion. Whereas in Germany duty to prosecute is the official and prevailing principle, in the Netherlands this is a right to prosecute. This gives rise to the fear of arbitrariness in judicial proceedings, in particular that state interest might override the interests of justice. In a certain sense this fear is well-founded where France and Belgium are concerned, for in neither of these countries is there an obligation to prosecute, while the public prosecution service is in fact an extension of government and heeds its policy. In the case of the Netherlands, however, this fear is less justified as the Dutch public prosecution service is more independent; moreover, this comparative autonomy is strongly associated with the professional ethics of the service's officers.

The Netherlands also stands alone in this respect, thereby reinforcing its self-image of always drawing the short straw. This image is understandable but just as inappropriate as the other member states' image of the country. It has already been stated that subsidy monitoring is also inadequate in the Netherlands. The annual report figures speak for themselves. They may be more positive than those for the majority of the other member countries but they are still far below Germany's figures. Moreover, the Dutch authorities themselves acknowledge that the controls are inadequate. The Dutch Court of Auditors, which is one of the most reliable and meticulous in Europe, has issued statements to this effect and compiled recommendations in line with the measures advocated by the Commission.[11] The organizations responsible for monitoring subsidies do not dispute these statements, but point to the organizational problems which they envisage facing themselves within the new relationship structure. This is particularly the case with the Dutch customs service, which had been reorganized with a view to the abandonment of internal border controls and was expecting to be able to handle the work with fewer personnel. Now, in connection with the monitoring of agricultural exports, the same European Union organization has asked for the service to be expanded again, with added justification since the Netherlands was granted a subsidy for this expansion. The question of where this money has gone provides a salient example of the managerial weakness of the Community's international organization. The Commission is of the opinion that the subsidy has been used to reduce the government's insufficient customs levels, while the Dutch government drily observes that without this subsidy the customs cutbacks would have been even greater.

All in all, the Dutch position is not a simple one. The country has a major vested interest in maintaining free trade and, as a consequence, good relationships within the Community; it is just as interested in a quick and flexible monitoring of goods to prevent stoppages in the flow of goods. It is these two interests which seem to be mutually incompatible; the tension between them reached its climax in the agreement already mentioned, namely, that in future

5 per cent of goods traffic would be subject to physical inspection. The Netherlands is a declared opponent of this measure which was the first resolution in this area since the principle of unanimity was replaced by majority vote on, incredibly, a Dutch proposal. The other countries were not firm believers in this measure. Yet they did not resist it, for two reasons: they feared to reinforce the Commission's distrust, and they anticipated gaining a competitive advantage. Even the Netherlands did not vote against the measure but instead avoided the issue, abstaining from voting and launching the so-called 'control mix' with which it tried to protect its own system as much as possible.[12] Nevertheless, a step back is inevitable in this field of power play, just as the southern countries are being compelled to take a step forward. This correction is partially justified because, as the experts admit, bulk agricultural products are administered with far less precision than industrial products, which are each given a separate number and are therefore much more responsive to advanced document checks. It is in this area that a concession will be inevitable. However, such a concession will produce new tensions as the Commission's threat is balanced by one from the business community which has already threatened to decamp to other ports if the 5 per cent control is actually implemented. These other ports will be Antwerp, Le Havre and Hamburg, unless the same controls are implemented there as well. This has been agreed on paper, but whether they will actually be enforced is far from certain within the European Union's international cooperative and competitive structure.

Germany

The countries in which these port cities are situated face similar problems to those in the Netherlands, albeit to a lesser degree due to the fact that the monitoring procedures are less advanced and the economic interest less important. This is the case with Germany. Even though this country may appear the least unreliable, based on the annual report figures and German legislation, it is not safe from criticism. The north coast ports are particular targets. These old Hanseatic cities tend to resemble the Netherlands, a visible example being the architecture of the old merchants' houses which reveal the community's mercantile tradition and the associated reservations felt towards the self-confidence and repression of a strong central authority. Herein lies the most important reason for the relatively late entry in the nineteenth century of such cities as the Free City of Hamburg into the German Zollverein, and by extension into the German Empire. The same is true of a number of 'liberties' which may have been incorporated into the body of German law, but are nevertheless characteristic of the north German mercantile mentality. An initial example is provided by the free port status of Hamburg which is beneficial in particular to transit trade. Another example is the *Zollhilfspersonal* who are authorized to perform certain customs formalities but are employed by a private company. This double function was probably a compromise to placate the old autonomous cities in the previous century. Now the days of such officers are numbered as the European Union deems this institute too unreliable. The German authorities are reconciled to this. It has already been said that the German inclination to obedience and cooperation is strong, while its interest in flexibility is less great, partly because tightening up this system will also apply in the Netherlands.

France

For France also, this last factor is a motive for it to side with the Commission's plans and not to openly resist criticism of its national control system. In comparison with the Netherlands and Germany, the subsidy figures, and therefore the associated problems, are somewhat different. In the first place, the number of reported irregularities is lower, particularly the sums which have actually been recovered. This may have aroused the suspicion of controllers from the Commission and the European Court of Auditors. Another difference, in which France resembles the southern countries, is the comparatively repressive and authoritarian character of its system, as demonstrated by the arming of its customs officials and the severity of sanctions which are salary-linked through a premium scale.

Such differences play a more general role in the negotiations associated with European integration. In particular, whether or not customs officials are armed indicates differences in the level of pacification and thereby differences in internal contrasts and in the natural character of each country's central authority. Most notably in comparison with Denmark, the Netherlands and Britain, the level of violence is relatively high, its internal contrasts great and the attitude to central authority highly ambivalent. As a result, unarmed guards and security officers are regarded as an invitation to aggression, while in the Netherlands the opposite is true. These socio-cultural differences, which play a role in such situations as consultations between private security firms, do not make the Commission's task any easier. On the one hand it has to propose measures that will be applicable to all member countries; on the other, it must make allowance for differences in national pacification levels and the feelings associated with these. As yet this problem has not been discussed, although it is interesting to speculate about which direction a solution might take. For example, the Netherlands may have to adjust 'down' in this area as well, which in the long term will make the carrying of arms by customs officers possible or even compulsory. That France might adjust upward has a precedent in the restrictions on the use of hunting weapons which this country imposed in conformity with European Union regulations. It may be that in the long term this civilizing effect of economic integration will repeat itself.

Belgium

A similar situation exists in Belgium but to a greater extent. The figures on reported irregularities in this country resemble those of Southern Europe. In many ways Belgium is the most northerly southern state. One characteristic of a southern state is its relatively weak authority, which was strongly centralized in the nineteenth century on the French model; for this reason, however, it proved unable to withstand the regional and socio-economic contrasts. Recently, erosion of Belgium's central authority has led to a political federalization of the country, suggesting that it would be willing to abandon its separate identity once the European Union has acquired statehood. Internal tensions continue and the government's authority steadily loses energy and thereby confidence. The customs service is also affected. The example of bribes has already been mentioned, and is confirmed by Belgian officials themselves. Mutual favours outside the official framework of regulations keep this country going, with all the opportunities for preference and patronage which such a system offers. It is remarkable that the Commission has not raised the question of this Belgian problem, as it has in the case of other southern countries. Apart from the fact that Belgian revenue from agricultural subsidies is a relatively minor part of the country's income, its role as host nation may play a part. The

Commission has its offices in Brussels where it has resigned itself to local practices in a number of areas.

Denmark and Britain

The last two countries mentioned in this context are Denmark and Britain. Both joined the Community at a later stage; their positions still resemble that of interested outsiders.

The relationship between Denmark and the Community is the least problematic. Clearly it gains a great deal from the European Union. Moreover, the competitive tensions between Denmark and the other northern member states are relatively minor. Danish agricultural exports are mainly focused on Britain rather than the Continent. Its stable national relationships have already been mentioned. In keeping with this, its figures for reported irregularities are similar to those of Germany without the recent downward adjustment. This is striking since, unlike its neighbour, Denmark is not dogged by a disastrous war past. Nevertheless, Denmark will also have to adjust to the new situation more or less in the same way as the Netherlands; this will include implementing the 5 per cent norm which Denmark also considers too rigid. According to representatives of the relevant Danish ministries, this adjustment will be accompanied by a less expectant attitude towards the Community in general. This shift in policy does not mean that Denmark wishes to turn the Commission into a truly central authority and is opting for scenario 2. On the contrary, Denmark reminds the European Union much more strongly than, say, the Netherlands of what it actually is: a continuous circuit of interstate negotiations. A good example is provided by the Danish parliament which, again unlike the Dutch parliament, does not anticipate an imagined development by farming out European affairs to the European Parliament, but has formed a kind of European chamber in its midst which keeps a close track of Danish government ministers in their European adventures. A similar sense of reality and a proper aptitude for political relations is demonstrated by the Danish decision that approval of amendments to the European Union treaty be immediately followed by a referendum, as will be explained below. This issue was barely discussed in the Netherlands, a country which focuses more on Belgium, Germany and France, as has already been mentioned. Given the history of these states and of Dutch commercial interests, such a position is highly understandable. However, the

Dutch control culture itself meets with little understanding in these countries. More could be expected of Denmark in this respect.

The same is true of Britain whose national characteristics have already been mentioned. Alongside its similarities with the Netherlands and Denmark, Britain differs in its nationalism which has a much stronger profile and is on strained terms with the trade liberalism that it also professes. An example of this is provided by Britain's long series of import restrictions for which the official justification is that they are for health reasons. This policy tends to appear irrational to foreign eyes and is an indication rather of national hosophobia. This is closely connected with the psychological characteristics of an island race nurtured on a feeling of pride in its 'splendid isolation' of the days when Britain ruled the waves. This *de facto* superiority has long since vanished, and security of status has become anxiety about status which, for the time being, strengthens rather than weakens this fear of contagion, and makes cooperation with the European Union difficult.

Government officials declared that the British attitude would become more positive after Thatcher, pointing to the counterproductive effect produced by the former Prime Minister's attack on the European Union. Living proof of this is provided by the Commission's accountants, who are also doing their rounds in Britain, demonstrating that the Brussels bureaucracy has gained in strength since the fraud problem was disclosed and that even the accuser – in this case Britain – is not completely innocent. The British authorities also acknowledge the shortcomings of national control procedures. They declare that they are willing both to adjust their singular judicial system and to renounce all forms of health-related trade restrictions. However, there is more eagerness to express such willingness than there is to implement any measures. Britain's aloofness when concluding international legal treaties is remarkable. This is certainly the case with the Treaty of Schengen, but also in a wider context. The less centralized and systematized order of Anglo- Saxon law in comparison with continental models is rather the reason than the cause for this lack of participation.

This defensive position is supported with the characteristic British blend of liberal economic and nationalistic arguments, with nothing being said about the threat which a 'free' European market would constitute to national achievement. This is why Britain is still the member state which is most entangled in the European dilemma. Britain champions a policy which, if pursued, would give free rein to the downward spiral of interstate competition envisaged in scenario 1. In practice the situation is less dramatic. British denial is strongest when the problems are expressed in terms of principles and therefore become political. Many of the problems are technical, as has been said, and can be settled by experts in interstate consultation. This is also the case with agricultural subsidies, where Britain's attitude has changed. Partly because of the surprising evolution of this country from a net importer to a net exporter of agricultural products, thus giving it an interest in the European policy, its willingness to cooperate has increased, just as it has in Denmark.

In practice, this change may signify support for whoever advocates a more flexible control culture; and this is the Netherlands. In this respect the Dutch have the most to expect from countries whose position regarding a united Europe is the most reserved.

CONCLUSION: THE HOSTAGE MODEL AGAIN

The interstate negotiations to strengthen control over agricultural subsidies are far from over. Nevertheless, it is clear that this endeavour to reverse the previous upward spiral is not based – as in scenario 2 – on transfer of national sovereignty to a new supranational European body. The gulf between the negative integration of market liberalization on the one hand, and the positive integration of the formation of state functions at the same level on the other, will therefore remain. The problems resulting from this are dealt with by setting a limit on the downward movement. This is expected to require the more developed national control systems to adjust downward and the less developed systems to adjust upward.

This conclusion agrees with that reached in connection with the Treaty of Schengen. In this instance too, the direction in which solutions are being sought appears entirely reasonable. The extremes of a truly free market on the one hand, and the formation of a European central authority on the other, are being avoided. Both of these possess the attraction of simplicity, but constitute too great a problem in themselves to be considered a solution in the negotiations. Thus Scenario 3, given the complex association of twelve states, illustrates what is feasible. Moreover, in all probability the new relationships will contribute to the suppression of fraud, so that initially the figures for reported irregularities will rise owing to stricter supervision, until the approach changes from repression to prevention and the fraud figures drop.

But perhaps this is too optimistic a picture so long as the actual conditions for fraud, the level of subsidies and the complexity of terms are maintained. However, even in this area of the positive upward spiral of agricultural costs, a movement in the opposite direction appears to be gaining strength. It is probable that the growth in productivity and costs is halting, and that the subsidies are being adjusted downward and perhaps being replaced by direct premiums on income. Given the interests involved, which generally have a national bias and in which France in particular plays a dominant role, this movement can only be gradual, if only to avoid jeopardizing the entire cooperative association. For this reason it is predicted that, despite some adjustment to the world market, irregularities or direct fraud involving European Union agricultural products will remain a temptation for some considerable time, even if control procedures become more effective.

To a certain extent control procedures have already been sharpened; further development in this direction seems likely. Nevertheless, we must conclude by tempering this prospect with a few objections.

Experience shows that the establishment of control procedures – when their degree of repression, scope, effectiveness and flexibility are considered – is directly connected with the development of the nation state in which such controls are exercised. The natural authority of central government and its mutual acceptance by the population are important factors in this regard. One will increase in direct proportion to the other. With control procedures operated between states, this development is less unequivocal or even absent. Such controls are generally found at a level that was more usual *before* the now familiar state systems were established and the law of the survival of the fittest prevailed. The European Union may be regarded as an unintentional experiment to provide the exception to this rule; the question is whether or not it is succeeding. Early attempts to achieve some kind of legal system at interstate level never amounted to more than good intentions, and only enjoyed success when one state indisputably dominated another. There is no such dominant party in the European Union and if there had been it would probably have blocked the formation of the Union.

Most find this absence of an ascendant state a good thing, but it may also lead to scepticism about the actual result of the negotiations. States make promises, but ultimately there is no central authority which can compel them to fulfil these promises. At national level this problem has sometimes been solved by one group violently subjugating another, or by the groups affected by such a threat joining to establish a federal authority. However, this kind of central authority initiated by violence does not seem to be a suitable option for the European Union. This has its advantages. The crucial disadvantage, however, is the situation as outlined here.

Perhaps the experiment will be successful this time, and it will prove possible to create a legal order which consists of states working together. As has already been remarked in connection with the Treaty of Schengen, in this case the compelling force is not a central authority which can coerce the others as a third party, but an implicit expectation shared by all. This expectation is that when one country violates an agreement in which it has no immediate interest the other country is bound to do the same, and in such a way that the interests of the first country will be damaged in answer to its violation.

Part III

CONCLUSIONS

7

EUROPEAN INTEGRATION

THE STATELESS MARKET: RECENT DEVELOPMENTS

In general, the European integration process is moving towards the direction of interstate or intergovernmental cooperation with the Council of (national) Ministers as the principal and ultimate decision-making body. This trend continued with the Single European Act, following which the Council's voting procedure, originally based exclusively on unanimity, adopted majority voting for certain areas. The power, more specifically the negative powers, of the European Parliament increased in line with this. This body acquired the right to block legislation by the Council but fell short of becoming a parliament in the true sense, being unable to initiate legislation or pass laws in its own right.

The process has continued more or less to advance without a dramatic and highly controversial transfer of sovereignty to a supranational European body, and without the downward spiral of state controls to which liberalization of the market would eventually lead. The European Union is therefore a stateless market which is not controlled at its own level but by the various states, united in permanent negotiation. This solution creates problems of its own, which have plagued previous alliances between states, and with which the European Union has been wrestling since its inception. There is a lack of decisiveness both inside and outside the Union, and an absence of democratic controls by the national parliaments, and even more so by the European Parliament. Other solutions, however, involve insurmountable difficulties, making the intergovernment option the only course open to those who do not want to turn back and remove the problem of state controls by reinstating the old system of national boundaries.

Internal conditions: the Maastricht Treaty

These developments culminated in the Maastricht Treaty. The position of the European Parliament was further strengthened by giving it joint decision-making powers with the Council of Ministers in particular areas. However, this right, and the veto, underlined the Parliament's negative function in contrast to the Council's final legislative powers.

In addition, Maastricht established the European Union based on three so-called 'pillars'. The first consisted of the three existing communities with additional responsibilities for monetary affairs. The second and third, new and directed, comparatively separate from existing Community institutions and authorities, aimed at a purely interstate and voluntary cooperation in foreign policy and defence on the one hand and domestic and judicial affairs on the other.[1] The treaty was signed by the governments of the member states in 1992 and was set to be ratified by the various parliaments in 1993. By European standards the commotion surrounding the treaty was considerable and represented a high point in public interest which had been rising since the Single European Act.

The federative option

It began with the preparations which were the responsibility of the President of the Council of Ministers, a position held by the Netherlands in this period. The Dutch government's position was no secret; the Netherlands was working for the creation of a federal Europe in which the member states would transfer sovereignty, in a yet unspecified manner, to a supranational body. Its attitude was clear. As has been repeatedly emphasized in the previous sections, the federative structure offers a fundamental solution to the discrepancy between market and state, at least in theory, and any party which advocates this option therefore appears to take the integration promise seriously.

Nevertheless, the Dutch option was puzzling. How could this country – or rather its government and the majority of its people's representatives – be willing to accept this, while other countries went into turmoil at the very idea? How could this country be so 'good'?

It has been suggested that the federative option was probably not an actual goal in itself but a tactical device which the Netherlands employed during the 1960s to frustrate France's plan to give the

European Community an intergovernmental structure that would expand under French leadership. This seems a likely interpretation of the Dutch position, and it is possible that this tactic was preserved over the years and brought into play whenever the precarious balance between the continental and Atlantic relationships were threatened by a Franco-European initiative. But there is also more to it, as is demonstrated by the preparations for a so-called European Political Union. The concept proposals which the Netherlands laid on the table were modest but nevertheless revealed Dutch aspirations. The course chosen was federative, as shown by the expansion of powers held by the Commission and the European Parliament. These were intended to function respectively as the European government and people's representation with genuine power of control. What was happening? Given the open rejection of these plans by the other member states, this might once again be described as a successful tactic. The federative plans did not proceed, and because of the high stakes no opportunity remained to make moderate changes along intergovernmental lines.

This interpretation, however, is too devious. When defending their plans the Dutch ministers did not give the impression that they were playing a game and that they wanted the plans to fail. On the contrary, they appeared to be sincere in claiming that the federative option offered the best solution to the jumble of problems. They were correct, at least in theory, but at the same time naive, since none of the other countries were willing to support this course. The Dutch were aware of this. The federative solution had not been a serious topic for discussion in any of the many interstate negotiation circuits. Why then had the Netherlands submitted these proposals?

A further brief comparison of the Netherlands with another member state, Denmark, may perhaps shed some light. These two countries resemble each other in many ways. Both have a long history as states, while their international position is modest in terms of territory, politics and economics; their national identity is taken for granted and there is little interest in national aggrandizement. The state machinery of both the Netherlands and Denmark is extensive, particularly in the care sector, and is comparatively efficient and democratic; relations in general are comparatively egalitarian, and are based less on command than on negotiation and mutual trust. The relationships are such that both countries might be expected to possess a moral and critical sensitivity which they would also apply to problems elsewhere in the world. This is certainly true at global level where by UN standards Denmark and the Netherlands allocate a comparatively large sum to development aid.[2] On the European platform also they both demonstrate that they are sensitive to the shortcomings of European democracy and government. In this regard, however, their differences begin to emerge. While the Netherlands praises the federative solution as a great leap forward, Denmark actually defends its status as an independent nation.

Why is there this difference in the midst of similarities? The answer probably lies in the realm of international economic connections. Both countries have many such connections, but Denmark – as we have seen – is more oriented towards Britain and especially the other Scandinavian countries. In the case of the Netherlands, however, the age-old balance between continental and overseas involvement has swung in past decades in favour of the latter. It is this difference in the degree of dependence on the Continent, in particular Germany, which has led through a similar moral sensitivity to two opposing strategies. The Danish defend their moral principles with backing from Britain and the other Scandinavian countries, while the Dutch can do little more than take the offensive with a federative 'mission', in which they project their own relations on to a supranational level. Both combative methods, however, clash with the intergovernmental course which has been plotted by the two strongest member states, Germany and France. This first emerged when the Netherlands submitted its proposals for European Political Union. The federative question was raised and immediately dismissed. There was great domestic amusement, with criticism targeted not so much at the federative option itself but at the lack of insight into European practicalities which the government had displayed. The speech-making community in the Netherlands did not apparently dismiss the option out of hand, and thereby revealed a European outlook which will not easily find its equal.[3] In the meantime the Dutch government licked its wounds, adjusted its proposals at amazing speed in an intergovernmental direction and managed as an alternative to strengthen the position of the European Parliament. It has already been said that the national character of the Netherlands has two souls: the preacher-moralist and the merchant-negotiator who endorse each other, contradict each other and sometimes also correct each other.

The Dutch proposals in a strictly economic and monetary field fared better. The plans for a European Monetary Union (EMU) did not constitute a break with the past but were a continuation of what had been set in motion within the European Monetary System (EMS): financial integration on an intergovernmental foundation.

EMU became a success, at least in Maastricht, where it had been decided to replace linking of the exchange rates with the introduction of a European currency within the not too distant future. To make this unification possible, a number of criteria were formulated with which the national debt in particular and the annual budget deficit would have to comply. An integral component of these plans was the establishment of a European Central Bank which was to guarantee the value of the joint currency; its directors were agreed and appointed by the national governments. The autonomy enjoyed by the board of directors was considerable, betraying the influence of the German Bundesbank which protects the German currency's virtual independence from the German government.

The compromise threatened

The success of Maastricht was uncertain, however. The treaty was clearly a compromise in which references to a federative solution were dropped and forms of intergovernmental cooperation in non-monetary spheres, such as social security, were removed or given a series of provisos. Nevertheless, public reaction was virulent. In the first instance the objections were mainly technical and in a sense predictable. The far-reaching intergovernmental cooperative structure lacked democratic controls. The formulation of fixed criteria for the national debt and the budget deficit, together with the independence of the European Bank, turned what should have been a political choice into a mere accounting procedure. Moreover, the question still remained of what effect the planned monetary integration would have. Given the differences in economic strength between the member states, the creation of a single currency would either rob the strong countries of their hard currency or burden the weak with a currency that was too strong. It might have been better to preserve the flexibility of the EMS in which, although the currencies were linked to each other, room was left to alter the ratios between them in consultation. This criticism was certainly not unfounded. Nevertheless, the governments of the member states dug their heels in. They acknowledged the objections, but having considered these item by item they reached the compromise to which there was no alternative, unless it was to halt the integration, so that the process which had been described as 'irreversible' retreated to first the European Act and finally, to the Treaty of Rome itself. Anyone who did not want this to happen – and none of the member states did – had to equip the planned market with interstate control procedures. Given the relations between the member states, 'more' was impossible; given the domestic market they had resolved to create 'less' was equally impossible.

But the debates began to take on a life of their own. They started in Denmark. As we have seen, this country shares the Netherlands' moral and critical sensitivity to European affairs, although it differs characteristically in feeling uneasy about the federative option and actually protects its national freedom of action. This difference was also evident in the Danish handling of the Maastricht Treaty. While in the Netherlands the usual parliamentary procedures were employed, the Danish government subjected the treaty to a referendum, with a small majority voting 'no' as the surprising result. There was international consternation. The experts maintained there could be no alternative to the treaty, apart from stopping integration; according to this logic the Danes apparently wanted to leave the European Union. The actual situation was different. Even though the treaty was in fact a compromise and the experts were correct in a practical sense, to outsiders Maastricht became the symbol of a greater Europe, with reunified Germany playing a major role, in which their own country would be swallowed up and become unrecognizable. Regardless of the counter-arguments offered by government and officials, this feeling prevailed, particularly among nationalistic conservatives and cosmopolitan radicals. The European Union might well bring prosperity, unite former rivals and provide a stabilizing element on the European stage; these groups were most concerned with the fear of being swallowed up by a large foreign power. Together they formed a small majority which brought confusion to their own government and that of other member states. What could be done?

The French referendum

François Mitterrand, the French President, drew up his plan. In imitation of Denmark, he decided to submit the Maastricht Treaty to a French referendum as well. Given the results of various opinion polls the risk seemed small, with a clear majority of the French people being pro-Europe; the President's actual motive was thought to be to use Maastricht to give his diminishing prestige a new boost. Whatever his reason, the fact was that for the first time in the history of the Community – aside from the Danish prelude – a public debate erupted which divided and united the French people in the same way as the Dreyfus affair had done. Here also, the fragile treaty was elevated to a symbol of a united Europe which far surpassed its actual content and was often at odds with it. Ranged against the treaty were politicians of the left and right, for whom Europe was either too small and capitalistic or, conversely, too large and too alien. The treaty's advocates, which included all the establishment politicians, defended Maastricht on factual grounds and stressed its compromising character. Nevertheless, the treaty also became a symbol in their arguments, but with a very different character. Maastricht was the future, the youth of Europe, victory over catastrophic division and petty pride. Moreover – and once again the old French ambition to link its own grandeur with that of Europe was reiterated – the new European unit could rival the other powers at global level. It was the President himself who went to the French people with these words immediately after the referendum, and congratulated them on the result in which they had pronounced themselves in favour of the Maastricht Treaty.

It was a narrow victory, however, so that uncertainty over the fate of Maastricht was not dispelled in the other member states either. A distinct example of this is provided by the considerable unrest in the currency market in this period; first the dollar fell rapidly and then the weaker currencies of the EMS had to suffer the assault of international financial capital. The German mark played a major role. The high interest rate in Germany, which was intended to combat inflation caused by expenditure in the former DDR, initially caused a flight from the pound; when this had dropped in value and been withdrawn from the EMS, there was a flight from the French franc. These events weakened the modest EMS system, strengthening doubts about the more far-reaching EMU treaty.

The authorities now saw the advantage in increasing information. The French referendum had in fact made it obvious that the compromise logic of the treaty was not the same as many voters' emotional logic. For example, many farmers had voted 'no', although there was no mention of agriculture in the treaty; and indeed their fate was actually safeguarded and protected within the European Union.

Despite the uncertainty, the collective member state governments maintained a closed front. A majority of French people had voted yes and for democratic politicians the majority is what counts. From a more objective point of view, however, there was another aspect. The issue was highly significant and could be compared to a kind of constitutional amendment for which two-thirds, not one half, of the votes is generally required. From this perspective the French had actually rejected the Maastricht Treaty; the treaty's future was overshadowed by this lack of popular support. However, this interpretation is too exaggerated a projection of national relationships on to international ones. It is true that the issue at stake was important. A state's own sovereignty was under discussion. But for this reason it was striking that not so few, but so many French people had voted for further European integration. This may not have taken the form of a direct transfer of sovereignty but at the very least it relativized it. As has been said, there was a strong emotional aspect to this vote which, however, showed an international outlook that is historically unique, particularly for the self-aware, proud and somewhat xenophobic France.

According to the 'hard' laws of market and state development, large groups of the population have failed to influence this kind of movement in the past. Military force and the threat of this was the decisive factor; when employed as a deliberate tool this method lay in the hands of social elites. For the majority of people, the coming and going of armies was placed on a par with epidemics and the equally fatal crop failures over which they had no control and to which they had to resign themselves in good times and in bad.

European integration was no exception to this, at least not the initial phase which had been conditioned by the course of the Second World War and its immediate consequences. Subsequently the situation changed. Thanks to the military balance between the power blocks and the international relaxation which this produced, integration became more a matter for the European states and their citizens. But even at this point, in the period from approximately 1960 to 1980, the European Union did not become a movement with which people felt, or did not feel, a connection. Progress was slow or even non-existent; where resolutions were taken it was the commercial, political and official elites which proposed and voted for them. This changed with the implementation of the European Act, and in particular with the Maastricht Treaty. For the first time in history, voters were asked if the criterion for national policy should no longer be the country's interest alone but that of a collection of countries as well. This wording was not used as such but nevertheless accurately reflects the core issue of the intergovernmental course – the relativization and relation of a country's own interest, not to that of a higher entity, and not merely to that of others, but to a shared community interest. Many politicians, both now and in the past, considered such a referendum to be unwise. The more enlightened argument for this was the belief that the majority would be incapable of understanding the body of arguments, and moreover would be inclined in an uncertain situation to opt blindly to maintain the old order.

In this light, it is not only the French authorities' daring which is remarkable but also the result of the referendum. Its very emotionally based character points to a European identification, or 'solidarity', and therefore offers support for the treaty of interests which the governments had concluded. This support is new and, within the relationships outlined here, will grow stronger rather than weaker.

The other countries

To what extent then did this animated attitude, so completely at odds with the familiar complaints about Europe, also apply to the other member states?

In Southern Europe, which for the sake of argument includes Ireland here, states are in many respects less developed than in Northern Europe. This is true of both economic and state functions, and of national identity. These countries can therefore expect a great deal from their membership of the European Union, while their emotional resistance to Europe seems less, with the Union even regarded in some areas as an ally in struggles for regional autonomy.

This also applies to Belgium, which for some time has been involved in a process of state disintegration, with a federative state structure emerging as an interim solution. Belgium appears to be anticipating a further stage of European integration in which the Flemish and Walloon regions would be incorporated as more or less autonomous entities, while Brussels would become a kind of European capital. This view probably overestimates the rate and degree of integration. The fact is, however, that politicians and large sections of the population are thinking along these lines. They are therefore pro-Europe inasmuch as it will contribute to solving their mutual problems.

Of the northern countries, Britain is the most distanced from Europe. Certainly in the period of Margaret Thatcher's premiership a form of economic liberalism was allied with a conservative nationalism, thus supporting a market without a state. This extreme view was modified, however. Even before Thatcher stepped down in 1990, Britain joined the EMS, which linked the pound to the other major European currencies. The new British cabinet, also Conservative but under different leadership, continued this policy and signed the Maastricht Treaty, although it insisted on a number of exclusion clauses and distanced itself from the social chapter. This irresolute stance was intensified when the pound was threatened on the international exchange market; the British currency was forced to withdraw from the EMS and continued to fall as a floating currency. The British cabinet's action was understandable, since the pound had been valued too high in a context of slow economic development; devaluation, at least in the short term, would promote exports. Nevertheless, the other member states protested, the chief complaint being that the British government had reneged on agreements; Britain had not decided to devalue the pound within the EMS consultation structure but had entrusted the currency on its own authority to the 'humiliating' effect of the free market. Irritation further increased when the British Chancellor blamed Germany with its high interest rates for the currency vicissitudes, and was not prepared to admit that his own weak economy was responsible.

This public quarrel soon blew over, but it none the less betrayed British hesitancy about the Community which is not confined just to the country's politicians but seems typical for the population as a whole. Even though Prime Minister John Major talked of 'our continent' when the problems were discussed in the House of Commons, in reality, Europe remains comparatively alien. This is felt less in dealings with smaller member states, such as Denmark, with whom Britain shares a relatively strong mistrust of Europe, and the Netherlands, which actually trusts Europe far more. British hesitancy is strongest in relation to the large member states, Germany and France; its traditional rivalry with them is considerable, and although both are democratic countries their hierarchical traditions appear to be at odds with Britain's more egalitarian attitude. This British attitude will not change quickly, even now that the country has finally accepted the Maastricht Treaty. The European dilemma will therefore continue to cause Britain the greatest concern. Britain is strong enough to delay European integration, but too weak to stop it.

Germany is the opposite of Britain. Germany lost the war, and is therefore still the weakest of the large member states politically and militarily, although economically it is by far the strongest. This combination brings out negative feelings in the other member states, expressed more openly than is usual in communications between friendly states. Germany itself rarely shows indignation. On the contrary, its national conscience frequently seems to be on the side of its accusers, with the result that foreign recriminations lead to domestic quarrels. A good example of this is the anxiety which German economic strength inspires in others, and which advocates and opponents of Europe use to give weight to their argument. Both are afraid of German domination, but for advocates of Europe this is a reason to be more European and to fetter their powerful neighbour while opponents fear that this will not bind Germany to Europe but rather Europe to Germany. That Germany is a danger is taken for granted, while the ease with which this judgement is made is as great as the expectation that it will remain unspoken.

While this anxiety about the German menace is more than imaginary, the actual grounds for anxiety are not strong. Germany has been exemplary in its European cooperation; this has changed little since reunification. The real danger is therefore not the dominance of Germany in itself, but fear of this which could substantiate itself, partly because the Germans are uncertain of themselves and do not trust each other.

This is true of German politicians and the population as a whole, with refugee policy being a telling example. Mindful of its past, Germany is contrite and takes in more refugees than the other member states. But this very policy creates ethnic tensions which recall the past. As a result, Germany's guilt complex continues. The Germans never seem to get it right.

The German mark offers the greatest national security, but here again the same problems surface. The galloping inflation of the 1920s was the prelude to Hitler's dictatorship; for this reason, custodianship of the currency has been entrusted to the national bank which, unlike its counterparts in other countries, operates with virtual autonomy. This unique mandate is understandable but at the same time it is rigid and authoritarian. An example is the way in which the German interest rate is set, and thereby the interest rates of other countries. The consequences of this have already been mentioned. The Germans can be reproached for being selfish, although they have shown themselves to be unselfish in their large-scale purchasing of threatened currencies, including the British pound. In short, the anxieties have not yet been allayed, even fifty years after the Second World War. Germany looks for its self-assurance in respect from other countries – but this is slow in coming.

Perhaps this sensitivity will decrease as younger generations appear who are less concerned with past injuries. But this point has not yet been reached. The guilt-ridden generations are still in power; they consider European integration of their country as a national rehabilitation, and they see it as their task to realize it. Hence the effort of the current government to maintain the tempo of the integration process. And hence the importance of a strong German mark which is extremely useful in gaining the respect of others, thereby increasing German self-respect. This is true of the government, but also of the opposition and therefore probably of the majority of the population. While the German people are divided over many issues they are not divided about their wish for European recognition, and with it recognition for themselves. For this reason the results of national referenda and parliamentary votes are of great significance to Germany – as well as to the countries in which such votes are held. Another country's 'yes' to Europe is felt in Germany to be an expression of respect; a 'no', the contrary. Only a few people are aware of this effect on Germany; French President Mitterrand is not the least of them. He involved the German Chancellor Helmut Kohl in his campaign for the referendum, thereby indicating, although he did not actually express this painful connection in words, that a vote for Europe was also a vote for Germany. Viewed in this light, over half of France voted for a country which had been its natural enemy for generations.

The two remaining countries, Denmark and the Netherlands, have already been discussed. Feelings towards Germany have also played a major role here. This was revealed, for example, during the European football championships which were held in the same period as the Danish referendum. The political resistance of 'little' Denmark was apparently rewarded when it reached the final and managed to defeat Germany. The anti-German feelings released by this event reveal more than simple sporting rivalry. The referendum result became part of the celebrations. In the face of these emotions, outsiders experienced astonishment and a certain aversion to this often coarse behaviour. Some people even cited this as proof that the emotional tensions between European states are too great to support further integration. However, this interpretation is superficial, for at national level the emotions conjured up by sporting rivalry are more comparable with the effects of the visual arts, music or literature. Sporting rivalry meets a need which everyday life fails to satisfy, because excitement is repressed. The same is true at international level where sport-related feelings resemble real rivalries but are in fact an imitation, even if real blows do sometimes fall.

This explanation does not, however, alter the result of the referendum. Even though the public debate was more composed than the activity around the football stadium, a majority of Danes did say 'no', which was a 'no' to Germany as well. Nevertheless, this result should be put into perspective, in the same way as the French referendum, for almost half the Danish votes were for Europe and thus for Germany, which is perhaps surprising. So there was no need for those wishing to see European integration continue along the lines set forth in Maastricht to feel sombre about Denmark's future. In fact a year later this was confirmed when a majority voted in favour of an amended treaty. They had raised their voices and had been heard.

In the Netherlands, the government did not submit the Maastricht Treaty to a referendum. The explanation for this appears simple. The country has no constitutional basis for a referendum, and there was no great public excitement about the treaty; above all, any excitement was not negative enough to compel the government to have recourse to such an unprecedented device. However, the risks would have been comparatively minor. It has already been said that the Netherlands' natural sense of national identity, its strong international orientation and economic dependence on Germany are the factors which determine what is probably a moderately favourable attitude towards further integration. Unlike the official government view, this attitude does not imply general support for federation. In the Netherlands there are similar feelings about Germany as in Denmark, with the probable result being that a large majority of the population is not disposed towards political federation. Government and the governed are therefore in conflict. It seems likely that the former will change its stance in support of an intergovernmental direction.

The European outlook

When at the end of this brief *tour d'horizon* the positions of the various member states are considered, the first conclusion is that differences in European outlook depend not so much on economic interest, which is considerable for all countries, but on national identification and the stability of the national authority. Where these are both well developed, as in Britain and Denmark, the attitude is hesitant. Where these are small and therefore less well developed, as in Southern Europe and Belgium, the attitude is positive. This correspondence obeys the simple rule that those with the least to lose have the most to gain, and vice versa. This rule can also be applied to the Germans, who may have less to gain economically, but still have much to gain from the European Union in another sense. Herein lies a major condition for the Union's existence which would diminish if German self-awareness were to increase and the balance between economic and more emotional interests were to shift.

For France, the connections are less clear. As a proud, ancient nation it has much to lose, and should therefore be reserved in its attitude to integration, like the other established states. But it is not; or rather, it is less reserved than might be expected. The explanation lies in its traditional ambition, in contrast to Britain, to tie its greatness to that of Europe, at the same time taming its old rival Germany. This urge has now become entangled with a more humane conviction that not only military and economic competition can lead to the achievement of this objective, but also cooperation.

The attitude of the Netherlands is also somewhat complicated. According to the rule applied here, this country would be expected to maintain a Danish or British-style distance to the European Union, which, in fact, it did, at least during the first phase of the integration process. Later it supported the federative option. Apparently the government was of the opinion that, given the national economy's strongly developed continental dependence, instead of simply defending Dutch achievements it would be better to project them on to a European level. As it turned out, this opinion was not correct.

The second conclusion from this brief summary is that, despite the differences, the European outlook is in general positive. The treaties which the governments have concluded for reasons of interconnected interests are supported emotionally by large sections of the population. While it is true that this emotional support is perhaps tenuous, it will gain in strength as the unattractive alternative becomes plain through information and public debate. Nevertheless, even at this point the European outlook will not lead to enthusiasm on a par with national solidarity. The intergovernmental form of integration is not the development of a state in a traditional sense, with state and nation continually being forged through violence and a heroic struggle against a vanquished enemy. Europe lacks this counterpoint and the associated emotions. This makes the process of integration somewhat boring and artificial, giving it the coldness of a contract, while national history, certainly in retrospect, appears impassioned and significant, although also pitiless and full of risk.

This does not mean that it is only interest groups that form the building blocks for European integration, and their interconnection the cement. What also binds is the feeling of being able to transcend the usual boundaries. For now national interest is associated with a shared interest with others without this being compelled by a direct fear of a threat from outside. This European outlook is opposed by national conservatism and cosmopolitan radicalism, whose dissimilarities, however, are greater than their similarities. The opposition is therefore too weak to halt integration for any length of time. Another force to resist integration is the scepticism which mention of a European outlook generally provokes. Appearances are deceptive, however, since a reserved and relativizing attitude is itself characteristic of a European outlook and gives it a special 'us' feeling.

External conditions: economic and political–military relations

In addition to internal relations, the direction of the European integration process is also affected by other events occurring in the world. This was apparent at the time of the Community's foundation, which cannot be regarded in isolation from postwar tensions between East and West. These tensions caused a number of European states within the American sphere of influence to achieve a measure of cooperation of which they were apparently incapable before. This cooperation was a hybrid: military and economic integration did not converge naturally, and the economic bond increasingly became an intra-European affair. Ambivalence constantly emerged within the swell of tensions between the two power blocks. When the threat of war increased, the Western European states sought sanctuary with the United States. Once the danger had subsided they sought sanctuary with each other. This was less effective, revealing the weakness of the European bond; within the postwar constellation the centripetal force of imminent war was Atlantic- or America-oriented, with the result that intra-European integration was denied this essential pre-condition and the development of a free domestic market stagnated.

And yet there was some acceleration in the process. The driving force was not a violent but an economic threat, which proved strong enough within the established relationships to set the integration process in motion once more. This new integration process did not amount to a transfer of sovereignty but consisted of interstate treaties. And this development is now less than secure, once again revealing how difficult it is to form a free internal market without its being preceded by the formation of a state brought into being through violence.

Economic relationships

Sooner than expected, the economic downturn which was generally experienced around 1980 subsided. Shortly before the remedy of a free internal market was administered, business in the European Community recovered. This reduced the pressure of the European business community on the liberalization process, although it did not disappear entirely, as was revealed when the French President was reproached by the business sector for endangering Europe's economic position by holding a referendum. However, this criticism remained a single incident amid a remarkable silence. A free internal market was still in the best interests of large companies, although the desire for this was less publicly expressed. This relative silence has been all the more remarkable, since the short period of recovery was followed by renewed stagnation in the European economy and, as in the early 1980s, it would be expected that the commercial world would demand an acceleration of the European integration process. What is the reason for this silence? Perhaps the answer lies in the growing realization that the free market is less free than the lobbyists suggest and is actually subject to interstate regulation. More important perhaps is the fact that the Europeanization of the market has coincided and in fact trails behind the globalization of the market. It has meant a loss of significance in the European Union for larger companies in particular who have now turned to other organizations to lobby for liberalization: GATT and its successor, the World Trade Organization (WTO). The relative success attained in 1993 in global circles reflects the move towards the Single European Act of 1986. However, the same applies to the central problem: the gap between market and state, with the one advancing and the other lagging behind. This disproportion is characteristic of the European Union and is the reason for its failure to correct a similar disproportion at global level. No support need be expected from the business world – except for the agricultural sector. For commerce, the principal advantage would be an increasing separation of market and state, unless – and this is crucial – Europe's ongoing weakness in the world market reaches such levels that companies start to demand protection. But that will not happen for some time. The liberalization of the global economy has made it possible for companies, instead of demanding protection, to move their production facilities elsewhere.

The victims in this shift are employees and employee organizations, who would not normally be expected to stand idle for long. But here, too, there is silence. If there is one national organization that has consistently failed to meet the European, let alone the global challenge, it is the unions. They suffer greatly under the European dilemma. Their influence is directly allied to that of the state, albeit with major national differences; given that there is no state at European level their power over events has been greatly reduced. It would be wise for such organizations to organize themselves at European level but this is virtually impossible since the unions are caught in the same dilemma of transfer of decision-making power. Their influence is therefore less than that of their natural opponent, business, which has managed to rapidly form intra-European organizations through various takeovers, mergers or by finding new locations, sometimes outside Europe. Companies have therefore undoubtedly constituted a driving force for European integration, which by its nature is less concerned with the problem of state controls than with the actual liberalization of the market. However, this force, once powerful, is now directed towards a global rather than a European context.

Political and military relations

Unlike economic development, external political and military influences on the integration process have changed less than expected.

This is curious. The principal factor here is the development of the situation in Eastern Europe both internally and externally, leading to the Soviet government's loss of control over events and the disintegration of both the USSR and the Eastern Bloc.

This movement is surrounded by misunderstanding. An obvious interpretation is that the Soviet Union was no longer capable of pursuing its arms race with the United States, and felt compelled to concede *de facto* capitulation in the form of far-reaching disarmament proposals. This version continues by postulating that economic weakness led to domestic discontent, which caused the regime to yield to internal pressure. But this is not what happened. The economic pressure of defence undoubtedly weighed heavier in Eastern Europe than in the West, but this relative shortfall was an old problem which had not forced the regime to collapse before; it is therefore hard to imagine that it was the main reason now. Obviously there were other factors at work when the new Party Secretary Michail Gorbachev gained power in the mid-1980s.

It is true that economic prospects began to deteriorate at this time. The actual conditions, however, had been formed in the previous period; these were characterized, as in the West but at a lower level, by strong economic growth.[4] This movement from the 1950s to around 1980 did not confine itself, as is often the case, to the economy in the narrower sense but had political and cultural consequences, too. The connection is well known. The more economic productivity rose, the more the scale of production relationships increased, as did the related technical and organizational requirements. This caused a rise in mobility – social, mental and geographic – together with a rise in the level of knowledge and general life expectations. Within this constellation, with the emphasis shifting in the Soviet Union from heavy to consumer-oriented industry, the differences in power between workers and management decreased. Moreover, a cultural change ensued after a period in which the establishment clung to the old structure, in which the new generation realized that coercive force from above had to be reduced. In the Soviet Union this was the generation which came to power with Michail Gorbachev. Without Western observers being aware of the fact, he had been active for years steering the regime in this direction from the inside, employing the well-organized and powerful secret service, the KGB.

In retrospect, this endeavour broke away from that generation's control. The rapid dismantling of central military and political functions caused the always delicate balance between centrifugal and centripetal forces to swing towards the former, so that the integration threshold was crossed in a downward direction. It seems likely that the new people in authority were aware of these risks, although it is certain that they underestimated them. As the first generation not to have experienced at first hand the divisiveness of regional or rather national sentiments, they underestimated the degree of centralized force required to hold the country together, and overestimated the non-violent integrating functions of an economic interconnection of interests and cultural identification at the level of the Soviet Union as a whole. Some felt this way, but for many people their aversion to central government was more intense than their loyalty to it, even when this authority reduced the level of repression. This lack of insight reflected the apparent unconcern with which they acted, at least initially. This applies in the first instance to external relations where the Soviet Union's international position dwindled rapidly and almost nothing was gained which might have been achieved through a gradual and tough negotiating process. The consequences were not immediately negative. The West soon had few remaining reasons to mistrust the new regime's good intentions, being astonished and pleased by the unexpected easing of nuclear tension, the regained independence of the satellite states and the reunification of Germany. At very little cost, the West gained what it had not dared hope for.

Inside the Soviet Union the consequences were different. Exaggerated trust led to snowballing disintegration which continued to accelerate when eventually countered from the centre. This restoration of force lacked authority and conviction, and opened the doors unwittingly to the motley group of anti-communists who forced Gorbachev's resignation; his power base, the Communist Party, was outlawed, marking the formal disintegration of the Soviet Union into a conglomerate of states, large and small. These continued their mutual rivalries, and even within their own ranks found it extremely difficult to connect the desire for autonomy with the importance of a collective binding agent, such as a single currency or army.

In this respect the movement in Eastern Europe appears to be the antithesis of what was happening in Europe. These states lost what the European Union was attempting to achieve, and vice versa. In the West this opposing parallelism led many to conclude that the splintering of state and economic bonds is contrary to a country's proper self-interest; moreover, it goes against the tide of history. The West's struggle to integrate was considered superior to Eastern Europe's struggle to disintegrate.

However, this criticism lacks a sense of proportion. It is true that history shows a tendency towards increasingly wider associations; the problem is that there is no fixed rule for where, when and at what rate this will manifest itself, and which component will begin to dominate within a new unit. In consequence every country, so long as it has its independence, can aspire to keep its sovereignty for ever, and that, when the time comes, it will wield great influence within a larger context. Moreover, and this should be stressed here, the contrast between Eastern and Western Europe is not so great, since the struggle for integration itself has clearly revealed how strongly attached the Western states are to their own sovereignty. In this respect Eastern and Western Europe are in a similar situation, and feelings of superiority are misplaced. The only difference, albeit considerable, is that the West is one phase ahead, and is endeavouring to integrate without individual state sovereignty being fundamentally violated.

Perhaps Eastern Europe will be able to learn from this experiment once the centrifugal storm has died down. But this point has not yet been reached. In the meantime it is surprising to witness the force which splits states, cities, villages and families along long-forgotten dividing lines. Such a movement is an attack on the state and thus illegal, by national and international criteria. But after the first success, central authority has to employ more violence, and the perspective shifts; 'illegal' resistance becomes a 'justified' struggle for self-determination. Generally, the social unit involved in the struggle is a reality, but it is always a construction as well. This emerges when the struggle continues internally, and only quietens down once every 'freedom fighter' is his own boss. This anarchistic nadir is the logical conclusion of the maxim of the right to self-determination; and this is its weakness. In reality this point is never reached, since sooner or later a new state arises which imposes its will by force, defines the new unit by decree, and turns the 'justified' struggle for secession within the newly defined territory once more into an 'illegal' rebellion. In Eastern Europe this struggle with weapons and words is not yet over. Nevertheless the contours of internal autonomy, or which entities will be recognized as such on condition that they in turn respect that of others, is becoming clear.

The fate of these new relationships depends partly on what the more established countries, in particular the United States and those of the European Union, do in this connection. Expectations in Eastern Europe are high, but, as will be demonstrated, the West will fail to fulfil these expectations and remain somewhat aloof.

More generally, it is noteworthy how little the recent developments in Western and Eastern Europe have influenced each other in a direct sense. The West did not press for disintegration of the Eastern Bloc, nor for the subsequent disintegration of the states it comprised. It did the opposite, by taking the old regime of the Soviet Union seriously for longer than did even its own subjects. The relations are somewhat different the other way around. Despite the new instability and the associated risks, the disintegration of the Eastern Bloc reduced the external threat to the West. However dramatic this reduction, it was nothing new and changed little in the external conditions to European integration. Moreover, as has been repeatedly said, a decrease in the threat of violence is not a centripetal force, and inasmuch as this threat increases, the effect of this is not European but Atlantic-oriented. The accuracy of this statement has been demonstrated within the new situation; for example, during the Gulf War which was won under American leadership. Another example is the civil war in former Yugoslavia where the European Union could do little on a military level without American leadership. This is not to say that developments in Eastern Europe have had no effect on the Western European integration process. Internally, German reunification strengthened this country's position and increased tensions within the European Union. Externally, the former satellite states are seeking affiliation with the West. They expect to gain prosperity from the European Union and, through membership of NATO, a guarantee against any renewed territorial ambitions by their former ruler or their neighbours. However, there is little basis in fact for either expectation. NATO limits its statements to empty promises about possible future membership in a Partnership for Peace programme, although Russia's role is as vital as it is unclear. At the same time, the United States and Western Europe have declared through the United Nations that they are prepared to defend the newly acquired independence of Eastern Europe. But will they actually do so? Past experience has shown that effective military intervention by the European Union member states is an illusion, unless this is part of an American undertaking which is organized with the endorsement of the United

Nations and, by extension, of the present state of Russia. This makes the chances of providing actual protection extremely slight; these chances decrease the further away the country requesting protection lies from the West.

The economic outlook is equally uncertain. Formal affiliation with the European Union is out of the question in the short term, given the major differences between the economies. Instead, economic and technical assistance is being offered, while the European Union's willingness to contribute to the stabilization of the new political and economic relations through economic sanctions and rewards is substantial. The democratic and capitalist changes have not been without their successes, at least in the more stable countries. But there too, the social tensions and problems have been considerable. Because of the size of the problem, Western help has been modest, while the European Union has maintained its protectionist barriers, particularly in agriculture. And the trade that exists appears set to produce a surplus for Western Europe. The West's attitude is disappointing to many in the former Eastern Bloc. They see the Union as a European federation which they would like to join. This hope offers them an alternative to what they fear most – a period of social unrest followed by a new isolationism and nationalism in which regression becomes a virtue.[5]

The European Union appears to share these concerns, but it is not prepared; and, given its own intergovernmental nature, it is not in an effective position to contribute much to easing the burden. This illustrates the relations between Eastern and Western Europe. It has already been said that their mutual influence is slight, while their dependence on each other is distorted. This was not formerly the case. During the Cold War the military destruction capacities were the decisive factor, yet there was a reasonable balance between them. With the disintegration of the Eastern Bloc the military power source lost in importance to another element, economic productivity, in which the West plainly dominated. As a result, while large population groups in Eastern Europe felt liberated, they found themselves dependent on the West, their enemy's former enemy, whom they saw as their friend. Henceforth the former Eastern Bloc states would no longer threaten violence, but only appeal for solidarity and request assistance, their sole sanction being the prediction that, if assistance were refused, the stream of economic refugees would become a flood, or that they would once again resort to military solutions. This moral tactic mixed with a breath of blackmail is usually one employed by the weak when they need the strong, but, lacking any concrete power, they have no other way of influencing the strong power's behaviour. The reverse is also true, not because the stronger power lacks the necessary force but because it has no need of the weaker power.

That the European Union has become so economically strong has come as a surprise to itself. The Union's development is certainly becoming complicated, but it is not directly affected by recent events in Eastern and Central Europe. For the Union, this part of the Continent resembles so-called developing countries; it is not 'the earth's people' but principally 'the earth's treasures' which excite Western interest. In the case of Russia this includes oil and gas – a treaty for the exploitation of which has already been concluded with the West. This is the Energy Charter, which was partly drawn up on the initiative of the former Dutch Prime Minister Ruud Lubbers.

COMMAND, NEGOTIATION AND IDENTIFICATION

The external conditions, within which the internal relationships are propelling the European integration process in an intergovernmental direction, have been sketched in broad outline. The rate of integration into what at best can be called a confederation will, however, be slower than previously anticipated, particularly in the second half of the 1980s. The reason for this is obvious. Precisely because the member states are dependent on each other and cannot exert direct force, being 'equals', they are taking their time to ponder the agreements and add all kinds of ifs and buts. The process may speed up again since Europe's position in the world market appears to have weakened, just as it did in the early 1980s. Perhaps the European Commission's 1993 White Book for economic recovery is the first sign of a revitalization process. For the present this programme of economic stimulation remains unactivated. This is hardly surprising. In contrast to the Single European Act the White Book is an example of positive integration, state measures at European level, and not negative integration, relaxation of state controls on trade. Yet it is precisely this form of cooperation that the member states avoid. And what is applicable for member states applies even more to companies. Business is more interested in liberalization of the market, and not, at least presently, in state controls at European level. Moreover, the economic scale has outgrown Europe so that the success of the White Book, Jacques Delors' final act as President, will be far more limited than the Single European Act with which this French social democrat began his tenure. Nevertheless, the plan exists and this fact alone shows that economic stagnation requires both stimulation at a European level and acceleration of the integration process. This positive effect of an economic threat, however moderate, does not apply to an external military threat; for example, if the level of violence in Eastern Europe or elsewhere in the world were once more to increase and threaten to assume its former proportions. It has already been said that the centripetal force of threatened violence is not European but Atlantic-oriented, which means that this would not accelerate the intra-European integration process.

These statements may have a reassuring effect. It is an uphill struggle for the European Union; nevertheless, the states and markets involved are moving closer to each other. Development itself is far from unproblematic. If European integration does indeed develop further in the direction indicated, it will constitute a social precedent, in that the market, not the state, will have been created first. The objections to this experiment are numerous. The most important raises the question of whether a governing force can be successfully developed in this way; a force which has sufficient democratic legitimacy on the one hand and on the other possesses sufficient energy to keep the process going. This applies in the first instance to external relations, in particular to the associated military functions. The type of expected development means that it is hardly likely that the European Union will build up a collective armed force like that of the United States. The European Union is therefore an economic confederation which can exercise influence in this sphere but remains dependent on the old monopolist for military attack and defence.

Internally as well, the interstate structure causes many problems, the major one being effective control on the activities of participants in the market. Previous processes of economic and political integration show how difficult it is to construct a reliable and efficient control apparatus while there is no, or only a weak, central authority. The European Union will continue to wrestle with this problem for years, if not decades. But if it manages at interstate level to build up an apparatus which is more or less equivalent to what is usual at national level in the more developed member states, the hard laws of state and market will be belied. It is not the competition–monopoly mechanism with the threat of violence that is the decisive factor;

it is the close, mutual association of interests that makes states appear willing to toe the line in words and actions. The hostage model is associated with this course, offering an alternative to the competition–monopoly mechanism. In this model it is not a command from above which constitutes the integrating factor but the more or less equally distributed chances of damaging each other's interests. This hostage model applies in theory in every social situation, and always between people who live together and are therefore dependent on each other. Its effect is decisive, however, when this mutual dependence is strongly interwoven, involving virtually all the major functions of living together, and is more or less equally distributed between the participants. Moreover, to be effective the mutual interests must have the prospect of durability; those concerned must accept the mutual vulnerability and allow trust to grow so that in future no abuse of this vulnerability can occur. The European Union constellation meets these conditions, with the exception of the military function. It is this weakness in the European hostage relationship which threatens future integration. The European Union is a market without a state, but above all a market without an army. In previous phases in the history of human social associations, this absence would be decisive and a market without a state would have remained a fiction.

In the meantime relationships have changed. The Cold War made it clear that, given its self-destructive level, the role of violence had reached a limit; the very self-destructive nature of the most powerful weapons caused the states involved to confine themselves to the use of less powerful devices associated with a more political function. It is not certain if there will be a further development in this direction. There is a very real chance that sooner or later one of the parties will resort to ultimate force, forgetting the lessons of the past. Nevertheless, the possibility must also be considered that even in the long term nuclear arsenals will not disappear but be reduced. So, despite all kinds of local acts of war, the world has entered a more pacific phase. If this development does indeed occur, the violent effect of the competition–monopoly mechanism is negated; or rather, it is transformed from manifest to latent, and the hostage model gains in conviction. This applies at a global level, and at European level. As part of this development the experiment of a market without a state acquires an exemplary value, since the central problem here will crop up elsewhere: how to integrate states without sovereignty being violently infringed. The European Union may serve as a model for the former Eastern Bloc countries, for states in South-east Asia, North and South America and, who knows, even for the United Nations.

This elaboration of the hostage model may be too optimistic and too ambitious, in which case fine thoughts about peaceful competition and cooperation, with their attributes of negotiation and mutual trust, may prove no match for the primary forces of violence and command here either. But perhaps the model is too pessimistic. It is based principally on economic interests, and on a clear awareness of these. While this approach is relevant, it also has blind spots. Homo economicus, to use a fashionable term, is a fiction since in reality people do not live in barter relationships within which they negotiate, but also in authority or command relationships, and solidarity relationships based on mutual identification. The latter is the relationship at issue here. Feelings of identification are no more fixed than the inclination to trade or command. To a certain degree they are spontaneous, in a biological sense. But biologically they are confined to those on whom people are immediately and strongly dependent, such as parents and children, and perhaps other family members. In the progress from tribe to city to region to state to nation, the scope of these feelings expands and constitutes an integrating force within the growing associations. These feelings also play a role in the European Union. On the one hand they slow developments down, as the function of the national state as an identification unit is encroached upon. On the other hand they have a positive effect, which has already been shown in connection with the French European Union referendum. Half the voters in this country voted for the Maastricht Treaty, thereby indicating that they identified with Europe in addition to their own country. It is argued that this kind of internationalism is nothing new and still comes off worse in the face of international rivalries, certainly when these are compounded with violence. Such objections are justified, and there is a great danger in this connection of allowing ideas to evaporate into idealism and ignoring reality. Nevertheless, it is also possible to be 'pseudo' realistic and to fail to appreciate that, if large-scale violence is brought under control, not only trade relationships but also identification or solidarity relationships will gain in importance. In any case it is justifiable within the currently growing relationships to supplement the hostage model presented here with the integrating force of interstate identification, which turns the calculating citizens of Europe into flesh-and-blood people. We have seen that this force is not similar to nationalism, lacking the clear counter-point provided by an enemy. This makes support for Europe less certain, but still constitutes an argument for nevertheless opting for Europe however vague, certainly if it proves possible to unravel the knot of tangled interests, which will soon be the case. Further developments will be slower than idealists hope, but these feelings will gradually become stronger, reaching out to encompass more people and, together with the tangle of interests, leading to a confirmation of the European Union, as Maastricht christened the stateless market.[6]

The test will be in 1996 when experiences will be analysed and the proposed integration will be formalized in new decisions. By then the Union may be fifteen strong, with Finland, Austria and Sweden the new members. Geographical expansion makes a larger, administrative expansion all the more difficult, an effect which also works the other way round. Here too, interests diverge, especially with regard to the countries of Central and Eastern Europe. For France, the expansion eastward threatens to undermine its position in the Union which is becoming ever weaker while Germany continues to gain strength. Perhaps these problems will lead to a two-tiered Europe after all, with France and Germany, together with the remainder founder members, accepting a high level of integration and the others grouped around the Union's core either closely or at distance. However, the other member states would have to agree if the continued existence of the Union is not to be endangered. The most likely solution will therefore be a balance between the two tendencies of geographical and administrative expansion and delayed progress in both directions, to the disappointment of protagonists on either side.

8

EUROPEAN CIVILIZATION

The success of European integration is judged not only by the level of state and market formation, but also by its consequences for the lifestyle of the people involved. The concept of civilization has already been used in this context, which refers to the self-control exercised by the individual and which, related to the expansion of the social controls of market and state, has gradually grown in range, stability and flexibility.[1]

This relationship generally holds true. However, it has found particular expression in Western Europe; with the accelerated growth of the social scale, power and control relations became increasingly centralized, while within this context people increasingly came to take each other into account in a more equal manner, and in that sense watched themselves more. This phrase expresses the context well and actually refers to what is better known as democracy, mutual tolerance, equal rights, collective care and individual privacy, in short 'the rights of man' which have become established since the eighteenth century. These characteristics of civilization were disseminated from the centre of this movement, in relation with the movements of market and state, so that Western European civilization can with some justice be called European, with – in all kinds of mixed forms and variations – global features.

AMBIVALENCE

The question of the relationship between integration and civilization is of both an actual and an emotional nature, in which sense it evokes opposing reactions. On the one hand, the pleasant idea arises – no matter how furtive – of a new grandeur for the old European civilization, which is authoritatively and self-evidently transmitted and disseminated. On the other hand, however, abhorrence is mounting, because Europe is 'too big' and threatens the individual national civilization or because it is 'too small' and as a new unity of identifications excludes other, less richly endowed groups of people. In these contradictory views the old tripartite division is to be recognized, of conservative and radical parties who oppose the course of affairs, and the liberal party which supports this. At the same time, however, the tensions are of an individual nature and they express the personal ambivalence which European civilization evokes. This change in position and esteem has already been part of Western European society for a long time, and whose actual controls, when analysed over the long term, show a rising line. This is generally not assessed as such by the groups and individuals involved, but is overvalued or even undervalued. The latter appears among those who lose power or gain power and in both cases criticize the prevailing controls. The first appears among those who are established and regard the controls as their achievements.

A trenchant example of overrating one's own lifestyle is offered by the nineteenth century, when Europeans spoke with pride of their civilization, which was deemed to be superior on all fronts to what had been achieved elsewhere. That applied to the self-control exercised by the individual, the actual civilization, but also to social organization and technology as a form of human control of nature.

This feeling of superiority was European, but at the same time had a strong national tint. It was British, French and Dutch civilization which was compared to the sun, whose rays released the entire planet from darkness, and it was above all the established bourgeois groups within these nations who cherished this gratifying image and used it to justify their expansionist drive in their own country and far beyond.

This triumphalist belief flourished in the nineteenth century and linked up with the European imperialism of that period. Before that, it had been different. In the Middle Ages the controls were limited, awareness of them was weak and the concept of civilization had not yet been 'invented'. The most important criterion which people in Europe used to distinguish themselves from others in their own minds was the Christian faith, and in particular the capacity to recite the 'Our Father' prayer, in whose name they paid respect to each other, even if sparingly. During the rise of the nation states and markets – as the concept developed and expressed the consciousness that to a certain degree people could succeed in gaining control of life, instead of being merely controlled – the feeling was not one of triumph. Manners and etiquette developed, often reinforced by the moral censure of shame and guilt. But this achievement was still no reason to take for granted a self-glorification in contrast to people who acted differently. A good example of this is the myth of the 'noble savage', formed in the second half of the eighteenth century on the basis of travellers' stories about islands in the Pacific Ocean. In this image, the savage was free of European moral inhibitions, but without being bad or base because of this. He was in fact 'good', but he was so by nature. As such he reflected the dreams of those who created him, the enlightened citizens. They strove for virtue, but the more successful they became, the more they also felt inhibited by their conscience. This tension sought an outlet and led to the noble savage, who effortlessly combined virtue and spontaneity.

In the nineteenth century the noble savage left the stage of social discussion, after turning from good to bad. He was still free, but his innocence became shamelessness, at least according to the nineteenth-century bourgeois, who themselves had risen from being outsiders to establishment and whose own lifestyles and standards appeared to them to be superior.

This certainty did not last long. In the twentieth century the word civilization acquired a strongly ambiguous charge, with the negative pole often dominating. It was a reaction to nineteenth-century Eurocentrism, which was increasingly coming under criticism. The evolutionist self-congratulation which had begun to adhere to the word made it almost unusable for anyone who felt the shame. It seemed better to use the concept of culture, which sounds neutral and does not evoke ideas of an evolution in which the European lifestyle came out on top. Unlike 'civilization', 'culture' is a word like 'fruit', which includes apples, pears and plums. These are not differently regarded because of any mutual difference in quality but by a difference in taste on the part of the person doing the tasting.

This non-committal position was not only a reaction to what was formerly the norm, but also expressed the loss of conviction in their own way of living. The question can be formulated as 'Am I living correctly?', which refers on the one hand to an excess of morality and on the other hand to a shortage of it. Recognizable here once again is the ideal image of the noble savage who is good, better than those who form the image, but without the burden of morality. Sigmund Freud played a central role in making European civilization problematical, giving trenchant expression to the dilemma in *'das Unbehagen in der Kultur'*. The human struggle for control leads to a new dependence, which is different in nature but not necessarily less oppressive. This applies to the mastery of nature, of human society and the individual impulses and needs, each with its own form of exploitation and repression.

Freud's meditation is not unique, but it is in line with the change of course set in motion by others. A good example is the interest in what would come to be called primitive art, in all varieties of music, dance and sculpture. These primitive art-forms link up with what is otherwise natural and therefore better, such as plain food, simple clothes, unadorned architecture, free marriage and free methods of child-raising. Consciously or not, all these experiments express the same idea. With the corrosion of the established European dominion and the established European civilization – with the two world wars as dramatic high points – new generations sought less coercive and at the same time more egalitarian relations, which were almost always packaged in a curious mixture of backward-looking conservatism and forward-looking radicalism. This was sometimes successful, so that behaviour became more relaxed and tolerant and self-control gained in range and above all in flexibility. But sometimes it did not succeed and the experiment got bogged down in the acute tension between increased individual freedom and mutual consideration.[2]

The fallacy of the norm of cultural equivalence

This movement continued into the second half of the twentieth century, and particularly in the 1960s and 1970s. The patterns were repeated and expanded. That was the case within Europe, where with lasting peace and growing prosperity, social and physical controls expanded, differences in power and class were reduced even further and in the battle against authority mutual intercourse became more free and equal, but for precisely this reason made higher demands on self-control.

Outside Europe too, declining power became obvious and the loss painful. Where it was no longer possible to win and defence became senseless, established Europeans also joined the ranks of the former oppressed. They indicted and accused each other of civilized self-glorification. They argued for the true civilization which considers all people, states and cultures to be equal and is not interested in qualitative differences. 'Partners in development' became the slogan of the United Nations.[3] This appeal is humane, but not consistent. What do you do if another culture does not subscribe to the basic principle and considers itself superior? Here the norm runs up against its own inconsistency.

Those who believe in the equality of different cultures also believe in the inequality of a culture which does not share this belief. This is a fallacy, but it is also a social and emotional problem which has found expression on many fronts. The intellectual example has already been mentioned. Eurorelativism set itself over nineteenth century Eurocentrism, which it accused of self-glorification. It was thus not so relative as the concept and its supporters proclaimed.

On a smaller scale and closer to home, the problem cropped up in the relations between the generations, where parents distanced themselves from the prevailing educational practices and wanted to treat their children more as equals. They found themselves confronted with the following problem: where their children did not naturally adhere to the new, more egalitarian and tolerant rules of the game, norms had to be imposed from above, despite themselves. This contradiction also shows that deference was not a step backward to a general human nature, but a step forward in the development of civilization, which parents had already taken but children still had to learn.[4]

A third and final example is the actual contact between various cultures, manifest in Europe with the arrival of fellow citizens from overseas, of guest workers and their families and of legal and illegal refugees. In the beginning, certainly, the influx of millions of people was met with goodwill, connected to the socially minded fear of elevating oneself above those one regarded as strange and inferior. However, this enlightened conviction had blind spots which impeded the view in every Community country, but most of all where the relations were more generally relatively egalitarian and tolerant. That was the case in the Netherlands. There, so-called benign blindness led to an official policy which made few demands on foreigners and gave them many rights. An example is the learning of the Dutch language and history, which was not made a condition for benefiting from social welfare facilities, the acquiring of active voting rights and the granting of citizenship.[5] The same attitude was present in the public maxim of political parties, the press and all kinds of pressure groups that migrants had a right to their own culture and that in this respect everyone should have equal opportunities. In all this the intentions were good, and indeed it also protected the public arena against the usual prejudices in everyday life, but at the same time it was naive and had negative as well as positive influences. No matter how tolerant people want to be, the fact is that the immigrants as a whole, and certainly in their mutual division, form a minority which is numerically and socially weaker and which will therefore have to adapt more to the established majority than the other way around. Furthermore – and this is the nub of the matter – this adaptation is not only enforced by the actual inequality in power but also by the norm of equality, which is expressed in, among other things, the principle of legal equality of all citizens, both men and women. The prohibition against taking justice into one's own hands is connected to this principle. However, this norm is not that of all minorities, so that equality has had to be enforced from above for its own good in an unequal manner.

Growing certainty

The fallacy of the cultural norm of equality is still a problem. Particularly when tension mounts, those who fear the most overt discrimination take the attitude that there are no qualitative differences, and that their opponents exaggerate those differences. In this way the political left overtakes the standpoint of the political right and vice versa, with as a proven method in public debate, either side confronting the other with examples of how these norms are broken.

A pointed and striking example of this is the comparison of the infamous Iran-Islamic fatwa which was pronounced on the writer Salman Rushdie and the ban on the wearing of headscarves by migrant children in a French public school.[6] The idea that these are two comparable forms of intolerance is misleading. In the first place, the difference in proportion is ignored, and in the second place, one loses sight of the fact that the French ban is derived from a general rule to avoid every display of religion, whatever it may be, in public education. Even though negative feelings probably did play a role, nevertheless, looked at from this perspective it is not the protest against the wearing of headscarves which is in conflict with tolerance, but the actual wearing of them.

Despite this recent example, in the last decade cultural relativism seems nevertheless to have lost strength, while the certainty of civilization has grown. An indication of this is once again the relation between native and ethnic groups. Partly through the many protest votes for extreme right-wing parties, the taboo against if not the official fear of discrimination has been broken and it is possible to speak in a more objective manner about the foreigner's duty to adapt. The same applies to social traffic in more general terms. After the strong belief in equality and the fear of being too authoritarian or too obedient, belief in the need for communication of norms and maintenance of norms grew.

This new certainty – in the commercial sphere but also in the state apparatus and in the smaller context of a family – was not just a question of acquired insight and conscious choice. Around 1980 the consequences of the economic recession which had already set in were becoming clear. Unemployment grew rapidly, and in its wake the power of those who could provide the scarce employment increased, while the power of those who wanted work declined. This brought to an end the long tendency towards equalization not only between employers and employees, but more generally, between rich and poor, old and young, men and women and – by no means least – in the judicial context, where the relation again became more hierarchical and authoritarian and therefore the degree of punishment more severe. The tendency was moderated in most countries, but nevertheless unmistakable, shaping the establishment of the generations of people who had risen in the previous decades. Radical sentiment weakened in favour of a stronger belief in the prevailing morality. The social norm of equality was hardly damaged by this, if at all. However, the realization became acute that this principle did not have the same power for all and was therefore an achievement which, if it was to continue to exist, must be communicated, maintained and if necessary defended, with the painful risk that in its defence the norm itself would be flouted.

National civilizations

In the same period that the consciousness and appreciation of civilized achievements was growing stronger, particularly at a national level, the process of European integration was accelerating. The effects were moderate, in the first instance, and also somewhat contradictory.

On the one hand, there were the more established groups of market and state who were primarily interested in the liberalization of the market. Insofar as they concerned themselves with the consequences, they saw the national civilization and above all their own lifestyle as reinforced, rather than threatened, by the European dimension. Europe became fashionable!

It was a different matter with less well-established groups with conservative or radical views, who saw their nationally cherished ideals as being in conflict with the European market. Inasmuch as they were even interested, they regarded integration with a detached distrust. However, the concern was moderate. Ten or twenty years before, these feelings had made other international frameworks into objects to be resisted, with the consequence that France distanced itself from NATO on nationalistic grounds, and other states kept a radical, legitimized distance. However, these feelings had grown weaker, so that European integration evoked less resistance than could have been expected on the basis of earlier relations.[7]

Nevertheless, there was some cause for concern, certainly if liberalization of the market were to continue without a proportionate expansion of the controls on it. But that did not happen. The member states signed interstate treaties curbing the threatening downward spiral of interstate controls.

This does not mean that the danger has passed. Certainly, for countries with relatively highly developed state controls and a corresponding level of civilization, it appears, as has been remarked, that with or without interstate agreements the controls have to be adjusted in the downward direction. An example is the judicial and political apparatus which in the Netherlands – but also in other countries – has to deal with a growing international mobility and criminality. This is combated at a national level by more repression as controls grow weaker at the Community level. The Netherlands' national interest therefore benefits greatly from a further expansion of interstate cooperation. The same applies to Denmark, even though here, as it turned out, this sort of interstate treaty is perceived more as a national threat than as a national benefit. Britain is also included in this context, which despite its natural borders cannot halt the new mobility or criminality, or introduce further increases of repression, unless it exerts its strength in the European framework.

But even then, if, indeed, intra-European cooperation is expanded, the process of integration has a dramatic effect. The national civilizations which in many respects are most highly developed and therefore the most vulnerable, have to damage themselves through treaty or through the free play of the market. There is little to be done about this except to raise the controls through interstate negotiations to the highest possible level, so that the loss of control remains restricted and furthermore is compensated by the gain in control made by other countries.

This does not mean to say that all member states will soon have reached a kind of European average. The differences may be relatively small compared to the rest of the world. In a mutual comparison, however, they are large enough to allow the process of harmonizing the many and extremely diverse state controls to last for decades, while the same process in the civilizing functions of these controls extends even further into the future.

The example of collective punishment

A simple example can shed some light in this area. It is derived from the many discussions which were carried out in preparation for this book with officials, businessmen and politicians, where a problem would invariably crop up at the end of the discussion which was apparently separate from the actual subject. This was as follows:

> Imagine. A teacher enters the classroom, sits down, but immediately jumps up again. 'Ouch,' he shouts and feels the seat of his trousers, where he finds a drawing-pin which he then holds up to the class. He asks: 'Who's is this?' Deathly silence. He asks again, but the class remains silent. What should the teacher do?

Solution 1

He knows what to do. 'If you do not come forward immediately, the whole class will stay an hour after school.' They remain silent. The punishment was carried out that afternoon. On the way home the culprit was given a hard time. If he dares to do it again, his classmates will tell on him.

Solution 2

The teacher hesitates. He is angry and thinks: 'Bunch of scoundrels,' but he stops himself: 'It was probably meant as a joke.' He looks at the class and sighs: 'I suppose you thought that was funny. Do me a favour and keep your sense of humour to yourselves.' He starts the lesson. The class pays attention. One of the children probably feels ashamed and thinks: 'Stupid of me.'

The moral of the story is obvious. The choice between two solutions is determined by the relations between the parties involved. Where the inequality in power between older and younger is relatively great and control relations are hierarchical and authoritarian, collective punishment is a proven method of solving the problem of the anonymous culprit. Where differences in power are smaller and control less hierarchical and authoritarian, collective punishment is in conflict with the sense of justice of all parties involved. It is not a question of consciously wanting the good to suffer with the bad, not even when it involves children. Teachers and other custodians of order have to bring the problem of the anonymous culprit under control in another way. Instead of authoritarian punishment they have little alternative but to appeal to the same egalitarian morality which makes these sort of tricks unsporting and tasteless or childish.

These kinds of differences have been dealt with already. The expectation was there that the chosen solutions would confirm the characteristics of the member states. That expectation was confirmed. All the Dutch and Danish discussion partners chose the egalitarian solution 2, while the Germans, French and Belgians chose the authoritarian solution 1. The British were divided.

Exchange of civilization

The question is, how will it proceed from here? The relatively highly developed sense of justice in the Netherlands and Denmark is of quite recent vintage. It is related to the social equalization in the 1960s and 1970s and above all to the expansion of education and other state facilities.

This movement has certainly been relatively strong in the two countries and furthermore has linked up with relations which had not been very authoritarian since ancient times. But what is to happen? The movement mentioned is now more than a decade old, and in that time control relations have been sharpened and the prevailing morality is again more consciously handed on and maintained. However, the abhorrence of collective punishments has remained, so that in this respect the equality norm has been preserved, even though conditions have changed to some extent. This also applies to the influence of the European Union, which does not intervene directly in the way that teachers and pupils interact. But indirectly, the relations are different. If the liberalization of the market continues without interstate controls, then – so much is certain – these controls will move in a downward direction due to the pressure of competition between the states. That certainly applies to social welfare facilities, which are expensive and do not directly strengthen the national competitive position. The same is true of general education, which is also extremely expensive and – unlike specifically technically oriented education – is only indirectly connected to the effectiveness of business. The consequences are obvious. Within the development sketched here the opportunities for power for the young are generally weakened, and the sense of justice, of which they are the object, will shrink as it formerly expanded. However, the assumption used here is not correct. The market is not left to itself but is controlled at an interstate level; at least, that is the intention. Therein too lies the condition which can curb and even stop the decline of the sense of justice in countries where it is relatively high, even if, in all probability, at a somewhat lower level.

The example of the drawing-pin is trivial seen against these major problems. Nevertheless, it precisely shows how everyday life is determined by broad developments and can be protected if those interstate controls are indeed established and carried out. The Danes and the Dutch have much to gain from this sort of agreement. It is a different matter in countries where punishment is stricter. These more hierarchical and authoritarian civilizations are also threatened, not by the operation of the market but precisely by the interstate controls which will ease the internal controls. For an outsider this is a step forward, but the parties involved see that differently. For them, the policies of Denmark and the Netherlands are too lax. This judgement remains correct, at least in the short term, as long as young people and others who risk punishment fail to adapt to the new situation and prove incapable of resisting the temptations which leniency brings.

These opposing interests of civilization form an excellent example of the hostage model. Economically strong member states have, on the whole, a more highly developed sense of justice, so that in this regard they are vulnerable to member states with opposing characteristics. These are in their turn vulnerable in their economic weakness. If we see through this conflict of interests, the consequence is that civilizing functions can be exchanged for economic help through interstate treaties.

These hostage practices themselves may not seem very civilized, but the effect is nevertheless that the civilization of the stateless market, seen as a whole, is preserved and will perhaps even grow. If these expectations are confirmed, then the generally ill-thought-out belief of established groups that the positive relation between integration and civilization will turn out to have been correct and both will mutually reinforce each other. If the expectation does not materialize, then the fear of conservative and radical groups will turn out to be justified. In that case the liberalization of the market will 'lower' the level of civilization, after which the mutual polarization in a national and communal context will delay integration and cause it to turn into its opposite. The likelihood of this regression – and this is greater than many in the establishment suspect – seems smaller than the likelihood of civilization exchange. In this light, the political fragmentation of Europe, and thus the national plurality of its civilization, will not be overcome but it will be made more controllable.

EUROPEAN CIVILIZATION

The political fragmentation of Europe has already been discussed. It appeared to be related to the Continent's geographically determined, high threshold of integration, which in its turn was an important condition for the strong development of the market and with it for the historically unique balance between economic exchange and state relations of command. The humanizing effect of this balance is unmistakable, because productivity has grown and influence and prosperity has been disseminated. After a few bends in the road, therefore, political fragmentation can be positively regarded. The other side of the coin however is the long series of wars which first came to an end in this century when the conflicting parties had peace imposed upon them from outside.

European civilization shows a trend of great contrasts. In the context of the nation state, mutual violence was subdued and in general mutual consideration grew. But in the interstate context violence continued to prevail and mutual slaughter of otherwise pacified people was elevated to an official duty and virtue. The contrast between 'us' and 'them' is in itself not unusual, but the unprecedentedly sharp contrast which arose in the second half of the twentieth century between the internal democratization and humanization and the external, technological–industrially fought war certainly is. Here once again, European civilization shows its ambivalent character, which is to a high degree determined by the violent course of political division itself, as well as by its humiliating outcome. The long battle did not have a European winner and led to a world-wide loss of power of the states involved and of the old Occident as a whole. That outcome reinforced the ambivalence of European civilization, which was perceived not only on reflection but also in the personal experience of those who were taken from home, school, university or work in order to do, by order of the state, what was forbidden in ordinary life: to kill.

The last world war ended half a century ago. Under American influence in particular, Western European rivalries have been pacified and converted into benign economic competition and cooperation. This has led to a rise in the level of ciilization and has enabled ambivalence to be reduced and faith in one's own civilization to be increased. Especially since the 1980s, social polarization and with it personal ambivalence with regard to lifestyle seems to have been reduced not only at a national but also at a European level. Today's quality of life – and not as it was or will be – seems, certainly in comparison to the once so imposing America, to be more appreciated by the Europeans themselves and by outsiders.[8] The same applies at a political level, with a central example being the collected states of the European Union. After the acceleration of European integration and the relatively strong economic recovery, the power potential, and with it the faith of these states in their own enterprise, increased. The disintegration of the Eastern Bloc reinforced its importance and led to a growth in awareness that Western Europe was no longer a loser dependent on its conqueror, but for the first time in fifty years, if not a hundred, is a winner to whom others have to submit. This turnaround refers primarily to Germany, but also to the other states. For these, it is even more true that they owe their slight recovery of status to the collection of states, the Community, which has itself grown in power and prestige and won a place at an increasing number of negotiating tables.

Nevertheless, these shifts, both in actual controls and in self-confidence, are modest and problematic. This applies to the state fragmentation, which is countered with interstate treaties but which has not yet averted the danger of the downward movement. That is also true of the military problem, which has not been resolved. Internal hostility may have ceased, but there is no European state, not even in the Union context, and therefore no monopoly on violence, not in the police and certainly not in the military sense. European civilization is based on a market without a state and above all on a market without an army, which for its ultimate protection is dependent on the old monopolist, the United States. This dependence is a weakness which makes civilization and its achievements vulnerable, but which also serves it.

This statement is in glaring contrast to the image of Fortress Europe, which is doing the rounds in public discussions. This bold metaphor is inspired by the interstate agreements to strengthen the external borders of the European Union now that, in principle, the internal borders have fallen away. These measures give the impression that Europe is protecting its wealth and characteristics of civilization more robustly, and precisely in doing so is flouting its own norms of civilization. However, that is not the case. Even if some officials, politicians and their supporters would like to see such a fortress arising, the fact is that the abolition of internal borders, certainly for the more prosperous member states, is only partially compensated. After all, the quality of some external borders is poor. The best proof of this is the steady stream of people who enter European Union territory without the necessary documents. The success of the new policy is therefore relative and can hardly be otherwise. The Union does not have its own army, police or customs, so that the protection of the external border is, like other controls, the problem of interstate consultation, where those who actually execute the controls are often not the ones with the most vested interests. The semi-permeable wall with which the Union surrounds itself is partly the consequence of the absence of a central state authority and particularly of a central monopoly on violence. This also has the consequence that those involved and their populations have difficulty in fending off outsiders. In this way, member states are forced to concern themselves with their fate, willingly or not, either within their territory once they are here or in their land of origin – in Africa, Asia and also in Eastern Europe – in order to keep them from coming. Once again, the outline of the hostage model can be seen, with this time the entire stateless market vulnerable without an army, and thus able to defend itself only by showing brotherly love.[9] In this context too the motives are perhaps not humane, but the effect certainly is – even if only moderately. The conclusion must be that the characteristic weakness of the Union, no matter how irritating it is for whoever wants to rule and control on this level, does not harm civilization in this respect, but instead serves it.

But the weakness of a market without an army reveals itself in other ways too. Even though the European Union has recently started to exert itself in international politics and the desirability of military integration is constantly under discussion, the experience up to now is not very promising. That is understandable. An external violent threat could be a positive condition, but that threat has actually weakened and if it becomes stronger again, the integrating effect is still oriented to the Atlantic. In that respect too, the image of Fortress Europe is also misplaced. The Union is not an attacking and defensive unity, and it does not look as if it will become that in the near future. The development is actually taking a different direction. Even though France and Britain especially – and perhaps soon also Germany – have a military capacity which is of some international significance, there the military functions are now limited and will increasingly lose significance, precisely because they do not operate on a common European denominator. In this way pacification continues within the member states. The strong collective emotions of a violent defeat or victory, also in their many symbolic forms, will become blurred and disappear or will merely continue to exist as a sweet or painful memory. This weakness therefore serves European civilization, but at the same time gives it an odour of hypocrisy. This 'vice' is inseparably bound up with self-control and thus with the concealment of elementary upsurges and emotions. But in this case the odour is particularly strong, because pacification is guaranteed by outsiders and not the parties themselves. In this respect the collected countries in the Union are reminiscent of a polder landscape where, with hard work and dry feet, the harvest is rich and fairly divided – also among the many guests – but where no one bothers about the pumping station. That work is contracted out.

This image does more justice to relations in the Union, even if there are reservations. The possibility has already been considered that after the end of the arms race between East and West the trend towards pacification will continue on a world-wide scale. In that case the pumping station or, in real terms, the American military guarantee, will gradually lose its function and European dependence its importance. In this perspective, the world position of the stateless market is stronger, its civilized attainments become less vulnerable and its competitive strength and – particularly in the agricultural field – its protectionism will become weapons which others will fear. Nevertheless, European civilization will then be characterized by a certain timidity, because due to a lack of political and military unity, it is based both internally and externally not on command but on exchange and to a lesser extent on mutual identification. These bonds are relatively egalitarian – no matter how harsh the competition and protection sometimes is – and assume a relatively high degree of self-control and are therefore relatively civilized.[10] They seem strong enough to propel the European process of integration and civilization forward on interstate foundations, but lack the strength to completely overcome the European dilemma and to impose a market and state.

The self-awareness of this civilization will therefore gain in strength and oscillate less between denial and overestimation of its own worth. The awareness of relativity and the sense of ambivalence between too much and too little control will not disappear, however. The European position is not strong enough for that and these sort of feelings are too closely bound up with a relatively high level of self-control.

This tension of civilization will keep people going, looking for a balance between the fear of failing others or oneself. People tend to be cautious. Perhaps the saying is true 'and the diffident man is, in the end, the more in control'.

NOTES

1 INTRODUCTION

1 Compare Council of Ministers/European Commission, *Treaty on the European Union*, Brussels/Luxembourg, 1992.
2 Compare Nico Wilterdink, 'The European ideal. An examination of European and national identity', *Archives Européennes de Sociologie/European Journal of Sociology/Europäische Archiv für Soziologie*, XXXIV, 1, pp. 119–136. This article offers a well-documented outline of the discrepancy between the European idealism of a few individuals and the comparative lukewarm attitude of most.

2 THE GOVERNING PRINCIPLES OF MARKET AND STATE FORMATION

1 The theory cited here on the formation of state, market and civilization is based on the work of Norbert Elias and especially on *The Civilising Process*, 2 volumes, Oxford, 1994 (1939 in German); Volume 1 was published earlier as *The History of Manners*, and Volume 2 as *State-Formation and Civilisation* in Britain and as *Power and Civility* in the USA.

Use has also been made of the work of William H. McNeill, *The Rise of the West: A History of the Human Community*, Chicago, 1963, and *The Pursuit of Power, Technology, Armed Forces, and Society since AD 1000*, Oxford, 1982.

Other general works referred to include the following: Perry Anderson, *Passages from Antiquity to Feudalism, and Lineages of the Absolutist State*, London, 1974; Robert Gilpin, *The Political Economy of International Relations*, Princeton, New Jersey, 1987; John Hall (ed.), *States in History*, Oxford, 1986; Charles Tilly, *Coercion, Capital and European States, AD 990–1990*, London, 1990; Immanuel Wallerstein, *The Modern World-system: Capitalist Agriculture and the Origins of the European World-Economy in the Sixteenth Century*, New York, 1974; Carolyn Webber/Aaron Wildavsky, *A History of Taxation and Expenditure in the Western World*, New York, 1986; Peter Singer, *The Expanding Circle, Ethics and Sociobiology*, New York,

1981. This work is of a rather different type. Its subject matter is expanding identification, and is more socio-biological than historical. Compare also Nico Wilterdink/Bart van Heerikhuizen, *Samenlevingen*, Groningen, 1989. This volume offers an outline of the sociological insights of which use is made here.

2 Compare Norman K.Gottwald, *The tribes of Jaweh*, New York, 1979, in which the history of Ancient Israel is described from a 'they' perspective.

3 Compare Immanuel Wallerstein, *The Modern World System*. Unlike Wallerstein the position here is that, because of the later domination of France and Britain over the free cities of north-west Europe and Italy, the advantages of political fragmentation, with its comparatively limited tax burden but with its high security risk could, in the end, not weigh up against the advantages of a free, state-protected internal market. On the other hand, the economic development of these free cities formed a favourable and perhaps even essential pre-condition for the growth of national economies.

4 Compare Carolyn Webber and Aaron Wildawsky, *A History of Taxation and Expenditure in the Western World*, pp. 270 etc., and Leo Noordegraaf, 'Internal trade and internal trade conflicts in the Northern Netherlands: autonomy, centralism and state formation in the pre- industrial era', in Simon Groeneveld/Michael Wintle, *State and Trade, Government and the Economy in Britain and the Netherlands since the Middle Ages*, Zutphen, 1992, pp. 12–27.

5 Compare Adam Smith, *The Wealth of Nations*, ed. by R.H. Campbell, A.S. Skinner and W.B. Todd, Oxford, 1976 (1st edn 1776), 2 volumes, volume 2, p, 900:

'This freedom of interior commerce, the effect of the uniformity of the system of taxation, is perhaps one of the principal causes of the prosperity of Great Britain; every great country being necessarily the best and most extensive market for the greater part of the productions of its own industry'.

As is well known, Smith supported a market as free as possible of state tolls. Like Wallerstein, but two centuries before, he showed the link in this context between the early free trade of the free cities and the city leagues mentioned in the text and the positive effect this had on the economic growth they enjoyed and from which the rest of Europe also benefited.

Nevertheless, he confirmed the later significance of the relatively large free internal markets which first developed in Britain and later in France. Smith had a sharp eye for the advantages of relatively undisturbed trade, but he did not consider the role of the state in imposing a free market within its territory.

Smith also emphasized the difference in the phases of Britain and France's centralization process discussed here and in the following paragraphs.

6 This highly compact description of the processes of 'state, market and civilization' can be found in a more extensive form in, besides Norbert Elias's work itself, such works as J. Goudsblom, *Fire and Civilization*,

London, 1992 and Abram de Swaan, *In Care of the State, Health Care, Education and Welfare in Europe and the USA in the Modern Era*, Cambridge, 1988. See also Paul Kapteyn, *Taboe, macht en moraal speciaal in Nederland*, Amsterdam, 1980 (*Taboo, on Power and Morality*, with a summary in English). For an extensive bibliography on civilization theory see Willem H. Kranendonk, *Society as a Process, a Bibliography of Figurational Sociology in the Netherlands*, Sociologisch Instituut, University of Amsterdam, 1990.

Compare also Chapter 5, especially note 3, Chapters 6, 7 and 8, especially note 10, in which the national differences in centralization, power relations and so the nature and extent of self-control in civilization, are discussed further.

Other works consulted include H.A. Diederiks, D.J. Noordam, G.C. Quispel and P.H.H. Vries, *Van agrarische samenleving naar verzorgingsstaat*, Groningen, 1987, which contains an extensive bibliography of works on the countries discussed; Henk Houweling and Jan Geert Siccama (eds), *Europa, speelbal, of medespeler*, Baarn, 1988; Barrington Moore, *Social Origins of Dictatorship and Democracy: Lord and Peasant in the Making of the Modern World*, Boston, 1966; Theda Skocpol, *States and Social Revolutions, a Comparative Analysis of France, Russia and China*, New York, 1979, and C. Tilly (ed.), *The Formation of Nation States in Western Europe*, Princeton, 1975.

For more recent developments, especially on the welfare state, compare Peter Flora and Arnold J. Heidenheimer, *The Development of the Welfare States in Europe and America*, London, 1981, and Harmut Kaelble, *Auf dem Weg zu einer europäischen Gesellschaft, eine Sozialgeschichte Westeuropas 1880–1980*, Munich, 1987.

For formation of national images see Ernest Gellner, *Nations and Nationalism*, London, 1983; William Pfaff, *The Wrath of Nations*, New York, 1993; Nico Wilterdink, 'Images of national character: five European nations compared', *Netherlands' Journal of Social Sciences*, 28, 1, pp. 31–49; Nico Wilterdink, 'Beelden van nationaal karakter: Fransen, Engelsen en Duitsers', *Amsterdams Sociologsich Tijdschrift*, no. 2, 1991.

For the developments in the level of violence and national differences see Jean-Claude Chesnais, *Histoire de la violence, en occident de 1800 à nos jours*, Paris, 1981; note the remarkably early pacification of the British Isles.

7 Compare David H. Bayley, 'The police and political development in Europe', in C. Tilly (ed.), *The Formation of Nation States in Western Europe*, 1975.

8 See notes 11, 14 and 15.

9 See Colin Crouch, *Industrial Relations and European State Traditions*, Oxford, 1993; see also Jelle Visser and Bernhard Ebbinghaus, 'Making the most of diversity? European integration and transnational organization of labour', in J. Greenwood, J. Grote and K. Ronit (eds), *Organized Interests and the European Community*, London, 1992, pp. 206–237.

10 Compare Carolyn Webber and Aaron Wildawski, *A History of Taxation and Expenditure in the Western World*, 1986, chapters 4 and 5.

11 Compare J.F. Bosher, *The Single Duty Project, a Study of the Movement for a French Customs Union in the 18th Century*, London, 1964. An example of the disappearance of local rights and duties in favour of the state system is discussed in Heinz von Dulong, *Entstehung und Verfall der Eidgenossischen Zoll- und Handelsfreiheiten in Frankreich, insbesondere in Lyon, von ewigen Frieden 1516 bis zum Tarif Colberts 1664*, Munich, 1959.

12 Compare Jean Cosson, 'La fraude fiscale et la fraude douaniere en France et les fraudes internationales', in *Revue international de droit pénal*, volume 53, 1982, p. 222, etc.

13 This is based on pacification in British society which had reached a higher level than in France and Germany centuries before. Note, for example, the typical, well-mannered British bobby with his truncheon compared to police officers in other countries. A noticeable difference, for example, is on Britain's roads; while there are fewer traffic lights, driving is less perilous than on the Continent. Compare also the text and note 6. Britain's 'advantage' has been diminishing in recent decades.

14 Compare John Brewer, *The Sinews of Power: War, Money and the English State, 1688–1783*, London, 1989.

15 Compare Edward Carson, *The Ancient and Rightful Customs, a History of the English Customs Service*, London, 1979.

16 Compare Ferdinand Grapperhaus, *Alva en de tiende penning*, Deventer/Zutphen, 1982, and *Convoyen en Licenten*, Deventer/Zutphen, 1986. Interesting for Dutch relations in a rather later period is Marjolein 't Hart, *The Quest for Funds: Warfare and State Formation in the Netherlands, 1620–1650*, Leiden, 1990, and *The Making of a Bourgeois State. War, Politics and Finance during the Dutch Revolt*, Manchester, 1993. See also J.L. Price, *Holland and the Dutch Republic in the 17th Century. The Politics of Particularism*, Oxford, 1994.

17 Compare *Leidraad Douane*, paragraph 22, in which civil service regulations provide explanations regarding the law.

18 Compare Hans-Werner Hahn, *Geschichte des Deutschen Zollvereins*, Göttingen, 1984, and Gerhard Köbler, *Deutsche Rechtsgeschichte*, Munich, 1990.

19 Compare Mirjan Damaska, *The Faces of Justice and State Authority, a Comparative Approach to the Legal Process*, New Haven, 1986; G.O.W. Müller (ed.), *Essays in Criminal Science*, South Hackensack, 1961 and George F. Cole, Stanislaw J. Frankowski and Marc G. Gertz, *Major Criminal Justice Systems*, London, 1981.

   An exciting insight into legal comparisons is provided in Jan van Dijk, Charles Hoffmans, Frits Rüter, Julian Schutte and Simon Stolwijk (eds), *Criminal Law in Action, an Overview of Current Issues in Western Societies*, Arnhem, 1986. See also Anton M. van Kalmhout and Peter J.P. Tak, *Sanctions-Systems in the Member-States of the European Council*, Arnhem, 1988.

20 This quotation and the following are taken from an anonymous *Voordragt van de Kamer van Koophandel en Fabrieken te Amsterdam*, 1934, p. 25.

   Dutch support for the British liberalism of the time is eloquently expressed in D.A. Portielje, *Geschiedenis der tariefhervormingen in Engeland*, Amsterdam, 1847.

3 THE ORIGINS OF THE EUROPEAN UNION

1 Compare for the outline provided here Godfried van Benthem van den Bergh, *The Taming of the Great Powers*, Oxford, 1989; William H. McNeil, *The Pursuit of Power, Technology, Armed Forces and Society since AD 1000*, Oxford, 1982; A.W. de Porte, *Europe Between the Superpowers, the Enduring Balance*, New Haven, 1979; W.W. Rostow, *The Division of Europe after World War II*, Austin, 1981 (1946), Herman van der Wee, *Prosperity and Upheaval, the World Economy 1945–1980*, Harmondsworth, England, 1987.

2 Compare B. Burrows and G. Edwards, *The Defence of Western Europe*, London, 1972.

3 Compare Kees van der Pijl *et al.*, *Een Amerikaans plan voor Europa, achtergronden voor het ontstaan van de EEG*, Amsterdam, 1978.

4 Works consulted include L.J. Brinkhorst, *Grondlijnen van Europees recht*, Alphen a/d Rijn, 1984; W.G.C.M. Haack, *Europese economische integratie, problemen en perspectieven*, Utrecht, 1986; J.A. Hofman, J.W. Sap and I. Sewandono, *Beginselen van Europees constitutioneel recht*, Deventer, 1993; Dick Leonard, *Pocket Guide to the European Community*, Oxford/London, 1988; Wilfred Loth, *Der Weg nach Europa, Geschichte der Europäischen Integration, 1939–1957*, Göttingen, 1990; P. van de Meersche, *Europese integratie en desintegratie, 1945-heden*, Antwerp/Amsterdam, 1978; J. Pelkmans, *Market Integration in the European Community*, Boston/The Hague/Lancaster. 1984, and J. Pelkmans, 'The institutional economics of European integration', in M. Capeletti, J. Weiler and M. Seccombe, *Integration Through Law, Europe and the American Federal Experience*, Volume I, Book I, New York/ Berlin, 1985; Sam Rozemond, *Nederland in Westeuropa, een plaatsbepaling*, Clingendael, The Hague, 1987; Dennis Swann, *The Economics of the Common Market*, Harmondsworth, England, 1992 (1970) and Wetenschappelijke Raad voor het Regeringsbeleid (WRR), *De onvoltooide integratie*, The Hague, 1986.

5 Compare Chapter 6.

6 I have borrowed the terms positive and negative integration from WRR, *De onvoltooide integratie*, 1986.

7 Compare E.H. van der Beugel *et al.*, *Nederlandse buitenlandse politiek, heden en verleden*, Baarn, 1978, especially the contributions by J.L. Heldring, 'De Nederlandse buitenlandse politiek na 1945', and E.H. van der Beugel, 'Atlantische samenwerking en Europese integratie'.

8 The national income of the former Soviet Union increased sixfold in the period 1913 to 1940 and in the period 1950 to 1980 three times, at least according to official statistics. For more recent periods, GNP grew 7.6 per cent between 1966 and 1971; from 1971 to 1976 6.2 per cent; from 1976 to 1981 4.8 per cent; and from 1981 to 1986 4.0 per cent. Compare Alan Pollard, *USSR, Facts and Figures Annual*, Volume 15, 1991, p. 118, Gulf Breeze, Florida.

9 See 'The economics of 1992: an assessment of the potential economic effects of completing the internal market of the European Community', *European Economy*, no. 35, Luxembourg, 1988.
10 Compare D. Overkleeft/L.E. Groosman, *Het Dekker perspectief*, Deventer/Utrecht, 1987.
11 For the changing powers of the European Parliament, the Council of Ministers and the European Commission, see Svein S. Anderssen and Kjell A. Eliassen (eds), *Making Policy in Europe. The Europeification of National Decision-Making*, London, 1993.

5 OPEN BORDERS AND THE TREATY OF SCHENGEN

1 This chapter appeared earlier as 'Kulturgerecht Verhandeln', in *Kriminalistik*, February 1991 and in Reinhard Blomert, Helmut Kuzmics and Anette Treibel, *Transformationenen des Wir-Gefühls, Studien zum nationalen Habitus*, Frankfurt am Main, 1993; as 'Civilisation under negotiation', in *Archives Européennes de Sociologie/European Journal of Sociology/Europäisches Archiv für Soziologie*, XXXII, no. 2, 1991, and as 'Onderhandelen in beschaving' in *Negotiation Magazine*, IV, no. 1, 1991.
2 This research is based on the draft text of the Supplementary Treaty of Schengen of December 1989 and on a series of conversations with members of the various delegations. I wish to thank Mr J. Peek of the Dutch Ministry of Justice for his introduction.
3 Here an attempt is made to adapt Norbert Elias's civilization theory about the development of self-control to the development of judicial controls. The comparison is as significant as the usefulness of terms such as scope, stability, flexibility, restraint and the expression 'controlled restraint' shows.

   However, the problems are equally significant. What exactly are the empirical pendants of these concepts? The problem is solved as follows. The extent of restraint is measured by the extent of police intervention and the length of prison sentences. The scope is related to the scope of the criminal law or of comparable regulations. Thus in my view the size of the police force is not related to scope, but to the degree of repression or restraint.

   Another problem is the flexibility of controlled restraint. What one person may see as the absence of control, another may see as the flexibility of control. I have attempted to solve this empirically further in the text.

   For a discussion of this problem see also Paul Kapteyn, *Taboe, macht en moraal in Nederland*, Amsterdam, 1980.
4 The proposition here is that the greater the degree of centralization and the smaller the social power differentials, the greater the scope of the judicial system and the less repressive it is. This proposition is confirmed by the four countries discussed here with the Netherlands in the lead, followed by Germany, then France and finally Belgium. Indicators are principally the prison population and the size of the police apparatus. The differences in scope are discussed in the text and

are augmented here with references to environmental and traffic regulations.

Compare for similar problems relating to environmental regulations Gerhard Dannecker and Ivo Appel, 'Auswirkung der Vollendung des Europäischen Binnenmarktes auf den Schutz der Gesundheit und der Umwelt', in *Zeitschrift für Vergleichende Rechtswissenschaft*, no. 89, 1990, pp. 127, etc.

The connection is confirmed by differences in the nature and extent of crime. In the Netherlands, violent crime is relatively rare and crimes against property relatively frequent, at least according to official statistics. This data reflects in the first case a strong sense of mutual personal consideration and in the second, large-scale and anonymous relationships. Compare for this connection and for the data mentioned Paul Kapteyn, *Winkeldiefstal in Europees perspectief, een vergelijkend onderzoek in Amsterdam, Zürich en München*, Arnhem, 1989, and 'Geweld en eerste hulp, een oriënterend onderzoek in een aantal Europese steden', in Nico Wilterdink (ed.), *Alledaags en ongewoon geweld*, Groningen, 1991.

Belgian statistics are the least plentiful. Compare for the size of the police force, *De politiediensten in Belgie*, TC Team consult, 1987.

The same relation is shown in the smaller differences in income and wealth and the level of social security benefits in the Netherlands compared with other countries. Compare Nico Wilterdink, *Vermogensverhoudingen in Nederland*, Amsterdam, 1984 (with a summary in English); *Een internationale vergelijking van de minimumlomen, de inkomensverdeling en de minimumuitkeringen*, Ministerie van Sociale Zaken, The Hague, 1989 and Sociaal en Cultureel Planbureau, *Sociaal en cultureel rapport*, 1992, Rijswijk, 1992.

The significant judicial and socio-economic similarities between the Netherlands and Denmark are remarkable. See the following chapters for further references.

5 In the sixteenth century, the Netherlands and Belgium of the present day formed an association of provinces which were ruled from Brussels by the House of Habsburg. The ways parted when the southern part withdrew from the originally united revolt against the central authority in the second half of the sixteenth century, after which the Northern Netherlands continued the fight alone. The conditions are probably based – apart from the military inaccessibility of parts of Holland in particular – on the differences in the power of the nobility and the burghers which were far greater in the southern Netherlands – compare Chapter 2 – and which were accompanied by regional and cultural differences between Flemish areas in the north-west and the French-language Walloon areas in the south-east. These differences frustrated later attempts to achieve independence, such as the plan to form a federal state in the late eighteenth century, which was blocked by the Austrian rulers of the time.

The independence gained by the country in 1831 – after having been incorporated in Napoleon's France and later the new Kingdom of Holland – was the result of British and French interference. As a result, the country was given a French style and highly centralized constitution allowing the Walloon aristocracy to dominate the country's government, which became not the object of identification but one of increasing resentment.

Part of the Belgian division is referred to in the text as 'particularism', which implies that prominent positions – such as judicial and university appointments – were heavily dependent on connections with political parties.

The contrast between Belgian relations and those in the Netherlands can be further seen in the architecture of cities such as Amsterdam and Brussels. Both are typified by the narrow but opulent houses of their burghers situated along the canals in Amsterdam and in Brussels around the market square. The difference is that in Brussels the urban architecture is dominated by aristocratic palaces which look down on to the market square from the hill, while in Amsterdam there was no aristocracy.

Interesting insights into the Belgian situation are found in Geert van Istendael, *Het Belgisch labyrint*, Amsterdam, 1989.

6 In the text the absence of compulsory identification cards is seen as a sign of judicial restraint. The criticism is perhaps that it involves a limited scope. However, this is unjust. Compulsory identification does not place a particular social action under judicial control with which it never previously had to deal, but introduces a new form of control.

   Compare also G.J. Veerman *et al.*, *Ik zal eens vragen naar zijn naam; vooren nadelen van een legitimatieplicht*, Arnhem, 1989, and F. Bovenkerk, *Er zijn grenzen*, Arnhem, 1989.

7 For the comparative success of the Dutch drug policy see A.C.M. Jansen, *Cannabis in Amsterdam, a Geography of Hashish and Marijuana*, Muiderberg, The Netherlands, 1991; K. Swierstra, *Drugscarrieres*, Groningen, 1990, and G.F. van de Wijngaart, *Competing Perspectives on Drug Use*, Utrecht, 1990.

8 Compare *Nederlands Juristenblad*, Special, no. 23, 1989, a special feature on Europe 1992.

   See also European Parliament Working Document, 1986–1987, doc. A2–227/86.

   During the examination the problem of emigrants from Eastern Europe arose, although the influence on negotiations was limited. See also Sarah Collinson, *Europe and International Migration*, London, 1993.

9 Compare Mancur Olson, *The Logic of Collective Action*, Cambridge, Mass, 1965.

10 Compare Godfried van Benthem van den Bergh, *The Taming of the Great Powers*, Oxford, 1989, and Norbert Elias, *The Civilising Process*, 2 volumes (first German edn 1939). The thinking behind what is here referred to as the hostage model resembles what de Swaan has remarked about the problems of collective action in the first place and in the second place the increasing interweaving of interests between social classes with the formation of the welfare state. See A. de Swaan, *In Care of the State*, Cambridge, 1988. The main difference is that De Swaan describes intra-state relations where the central functions have already been established, whereas *The Stateless Market* concerns interstate relations

where these are absent. In the first case the integrating functions of the hostage model are supplementary. In the second, they are independent and therefore more important.

In addition, it is clear that both in *The Stateless Market* and in De Swaan's work the development of human identification or solidarity is related to increasing interwoven interests and the mutual vulnerability which results. I feel my concept of identification to have more to do with moral emotions, even when the scope suddenly changes, and that it is less directly linked to the rationality of conscious interests of the parties involved. In this light De Swaan is more loyal to the so-called rational choice theory which in my opinion credits people with more rational intelligence than they deserve. Moreover, this theory is too exclusively economic–rational and does little justice to other forms of rationality intended to safeguard or acquire status or identity. Compare Chapter 7, p. 153 and Chapter 8, p. 172.

6 AGRICULTURAL POLICY AND AGRICULTURAL FRAUD

1 The research dealt with here is based on discussions with the following people in addition to the works mentioned in the footnotes:

- civil servants at the European Commission in Brussels;
- civil servants at the European Treasury in Luxembourg;
- civil servants at the Ministries of Agriculture and Finance in Belgium, Denmark, Germany, France, Britain and the Netherlands;
- civil servants at the customs department in Rotterdam;
- civil servants at the Central Investigation and Information Department in The Hague;
- representatives of the Rotterdam Chamber of Commerce;
- the Ministry of Justice in Rotterdam;
- representatives of companies dealing in agricultural produce;
- representatives of transport companies.

The research took place in 1991/1992. I would like to thank Arnold Peeters, Dutch civil servant with the UCLAF, a department of the European Commission concerned especially with combating fraud in an EU context, for his help.

2 The Official Journal of the European Communities' Treasury, special report no. 2/90 on the 'Beheer en de Controle over het Beheer en de Controle van Uitvoerrestituties vergezeld van de Antwoorden van de Commissie', 90/C 133/01, 31 May 1990.

3 This concerned grain dealer Richco, established in, among other places, Rotterdam.

4 Journalist publications about EU fraud include Hort Keller and Gerhard Maier, *Skandal im Kühlhaus, dubiöse Geschäfte in der EG*, Bonn Aktuel, 1987; Nigel Tutt, *Europe on the Fiddle: the Common Market Scandal*, Helm, London, 1989 (Dutch translation *Europa knoeit, de vuile was van de Europese Gemeenschap*, Amsterdam, 1990).

Various academic works include Klaus Tiedemann, 'Reform des Sanktionswesens auf dem Gebiete der Agrarmarktes der EWG', in *Strafrecht, Unternehmensrecht, Auswaltsrechts, Festschrift für Gerd Pfeiffer*, reprinted by Otto Friedrich, Cologne, 1988; 'Teatrum Criminologicum Brittanicum', In *Festschrift oder nicht? 25 Jahre Kolloquien des Südwestdeutsches Kriminologisches Institutes*, Freiburg, reprinted 1989; Dietrich Oehler, 'Fragen zum Strafrecht der Europäischen Gemeinschaft', in *Festschrift für Hans-Heinrich Jescheck zum 70 Geburtstag*, 2nd Halbband, Berlin, 1985; Michel Massé, 'Infractions contre l'ordre financier', *Revue de science criminelle et de droit pénal comparé*, III, 1989, pp. 527–536; Mireille Delmas-Marty and Evelyne Roche-Pire, *Criminalité des affaires et marché commun. Quelques aspects*, Paris, 1982; R.A.F. Gerding, 'Internationale fraude', in *Internationalisering van het strafrecht*, Nijmegen, 1986; A.M.M. Orie, 'Internationale opsporing', in *Internationalisering van het strafrecht*, Nijmegen, 1986; J.A.E. Vervaele, *Fraud against the Community; The Need for European Fraud Legislation*, European Monographs no. 3, Deventer, 1993, with extensive judicial bibliography, E. Mennens, 'Fraudebestrijding in de Europese Gemeenschap', in *Sociaal-economische wetgeving*, 1986, pp. 624–640 and C.S.P. Harding, 'The European communities and control of criminal business activities', in *International and Comparative Law Quarterly*, 1982, pp. 246–262.

5 Various works on the foundation of the European Community and the role of agriculture include John S. Marsh and Pamela J. Swanney, *Agriculture and the European Community*, London, 1980; P. Coffey (ed.), *Main Economic Policy Areas of the EEC*, The Hague, 1983; G. Meester and D. Strijker, *Het Europees landbouwbeleid voorbij de scheidslijn van zelfvoorziening*, LEI/WRR, The Hague, 1985; *De onvoltooide integratie*, WRR, The Hague, 1986; P.C. van den Noort, 'De realiteit van de Europese landbouwprotectie', in W.G.C.M. Haack (ed.), *Europese economische integratie, problemen en perspectieven*, Utrecht, 1986, pp. 204–216; J. Pelkmans (ed.), *Can the CAP be Reformed?*, IEAP, Maastricht, 1985, and W.J. Bijman, 'Het gemeenschappelijke landbouwbeleid van de EG', in Henk Houweling and Jan Geert Siccama (eds), *Europa, speelbal of medespeler*, Baarn, 1988, pp. 88–108.

The picture presented here is based in part on an interview with former Dutch Minister of Agriculture and first Community agricultural commissioner Sicco Mansholt. He emphasized the Franco-German compromise between agricultural protection on the one hand and relatively low levels for protection of industrial products on the other. In addition, he pointed to the interests of the Commission as chairman of the interstate negotiations within the Community which allowed him to withdraw a proposal if it had not been accepted in a particular form. This power is supposed at a given moment to have convinced France to drop its further demands and to vote for the proposals on the table.

6 Compare A.W. de Porte, *Europe Between the Superpowers, the Enduring Balance*, New Haven/London, 1979.

7 Compare Klaus Tiedemann in *Festschrift oder nicht?*

8 Compare note 4, Klaus Tiedemann in *Festschrift oder nicht?* and J.A.E. Vervaele, *Fraud against the Community*.

For the history of customs services in Germany, France, the Netherlands and Britain compare Chapter 2.

9 *Report drawn up on behalf of the Committee on Budgetary Control on preventing and combatting fraud against EC-budget in a post-1992 Europe*, report by Piet Dankert, 23 March 1989. Compare also J.A.E. Vervaele, *Fraud against the Community*. Chapter 2.

10 A remarkable example of former Prime Minister Margaret Thatcher's style is the speech she made in 1988 in Ghent not long after the British House of Lords had called and examined the German specialist Klaus Tiedemann. See Klaus Tiedemann in *Festschrift oder nicht?*

11 Compare *Tweede Kamer der Staten-Generaal, vergaderjaar 1990–1991, 22 158, Juniverslag van de Algemene Rekenkamer paragraaf 9,2*, pp. 46–54.

A comparison between various national Courts of Audits is found in Ruud Berndsen, 'Report on the 28th Conference of European Community Courts of Audit', *International Journal of Government Auditing*, January 1990.

12 Compare *Tweede Kamer der Staten-Generaal, vergaderjaar 1989–1990, 21 098, Onregelmatigheden in de zuivelsector (NIZO-procédé)*.

7   EUROPEAN INTEGRATION

1 The amount of paperwork involved in this treaty weighs several kilos and few of the ministers concerned will have studied the material in its entirety. That applies equally to the interested outsiders who were provided with a handy 253-page summary produced for the Commission and the Council of Ministers but for the contents of which they accepted no responsibility. The question remains whether there is anyone who knows exactly what was decided at Maastricht. Compare Council of Ministers/European Commission, *Treaty on the Europese Union*, Brussels/Luxembourg, 1992. An interesting preliminary study on EMU is P. De Grauwe *et al.*, *De Europese monetaire integratie: vier visies*, WRR, The Hague, 1989. See also Svein S. Anderssen and Kjell A. Eliassen (eds), *Making Policy in Europe. The Europeification of National Decision-making*, London, 1993.

2 Compare Chapter 5, note 3, in which other similarities between the Netherlands and Denmark are discussed.

3 The fact that public opinion is not against the federal option does not mean that it is in favour of it either. The dominating sentiment is scepticism, and this is not just a recent development. Compare Europa, *Eenmaal andermaal*, Amsterdam, 1985, in which J.L. Heldring, M. Brands, B. Tromp, G. van Benthem van den Bergh and K. Koch express this view. Another sceptical voice is that of Nico Wilterdink in 'Europa als ideaal', in *Het Europees labyrint*, Amsterdam, 1991; A. de Swaan in *de Volkskrant* of 29 June 1991 and Ben Knapen and Arend Jan Boekestijn in *NRC-Handelsblad* on 3 and 15 December 1990 respectively.

This observation was noted earlier in Paul Kapteyn, 'De VS van Europa, een ideaal in de politiek', in *Socialisme en democratie*, no. 11, 1991.

For scepticism in the Netherlands see Bart Tromp, *Het einde van de politiek?* Schoonhoven, 1990, in which the discrepancy between market and state is discussed. Relevant in this context is Bart Tromp, *Nederlands cultuurbeleid en de Europese gemeenschappen, een beleidsverkenning*, Zeist, 1989. In contrast see Johan Galtung, *The European Community, a Superpower in the Making*, Oslo, 1973, in which state formation is seen as the natural result of market formation. The writer's view has remained unchanged since the appearance of this volume, as testified in his introductory speech during the 'First European Conference of Sociology', Vienna, 26–29 August 1992.

4 Compare Chapter 3, note 8.

5 The hope in Central Europe for a large European federation dates from before the war and was expressed, among others, by the Czech statesman and sociologist Thomas Masaryk. Compare his *Das neue Europa*, 1924.

6 Compare Chapter 5, p. 91 and note 10; also Chapter 8, p. 172.

8 EUROPEAN CIVILIZATION

1 Compare for the following observations Paul Kapteyn, *Taboe, macht en moraal in Nederland*, Amsterdam, 1980, Chapter 2 *en passim.*

2 Recent problems relating to 'self-control' form the theme of the work of Cas Wouters. Compare *Van minnen en sterven; informalisering, veranderingen in de omgangsvormen sinds 1930, i.h.b. in Nederland*, Amsterdam, 1990. Compare also Paul Kapteyn, *Taboe, macht en moraal in Nederland*, and *In de speeltuin Nederland, over gezagsveranderingen tussen ouderen en jongeren*, Amsterdam, 1985.

3 *Partners in Development:* Report of the Commission on international development chairman Lester Pearson, London, 1969.

4 Compare Paul Kapteyn, *Taboe, macht en moraal in Nederland*, especially Chapter 4.

5 Typical of Dutch attitudes in this context is that official statistics on the proportion of immigrants involved in crime as a whole are not available for research.

6 Compare Frans Bovenkerk, *Hedendaags kwaad, criminologische opstellen*, Amsterdam, 1992, p. 61, and 'Misdaad en de multi-ethnische samenleving', in *Justitiële verkenningen*, 1990, no. 5.

7 A good example of a 'radical' criticism of the EU is Herman Verbeek, *Economie als wereldoorlog*, Kampen, 1990.

8 The depolarization of Western Europe is shown by the relative consensus between the traditional political parties about almost every major issue in almost every member state of the EU. Directly linked to this, left- and right-wing radical groups have lost ground compared to before and after the Second World War, despite the rise of the extreme Right in response to increasing immigration.

9 This declaration of 'solidarity' or 'brotherly love' is remarkably similar to what A. de Swaan writes about the rise of the Welfare State. See Chapter 5, p. 91 and note 10 and Chapter 7, p. 153. That applies in a

general way to what is referred to here as the hostage model, although with the proviso that De Swaan is concerned with state, and in this book interstate relations. Moreover, the hostage model, with its explanation in terms of 'mutual vulnerability through the interweaving of interests', is augmented in this volume by the more emotive component of mutual identification.

10 As noted earlier, the discussion here is directed very much towards the state and civilization theory of Norbert Elias. As is clear from the text, use has also been made of the classical division into 'order, exchange and identification relationships'. This division can also be found in the well-known three-way split into conservative, liberal and radical ideologies, in Talcott Parsons' functional system, which in fact uses a four-way division (see his *The Social System*, London, 1964) and Amitai Etzioni's division in the context of organizational sociology (see his *A Comparative Analysis of Complex Organisations*, New York, 1975).

In this book the three concepts refer to three different controls which people exercise over each other. These are related to differences in the nature of people's mutual dependence and thus to mutual power differences. If the level of dependence is small, the distribution unequal and the discrepancy in power great, control will depend more on orders and obedience and will be supported by a 'hierarchic solidarity'. As shown in civilization theory the self-control of those concerned will be relatively limited. The greater the scale of dependence, the less unequal the division and so the smaller the difference in power, the more control will be based on exchange and on the identification of 'egalitarian solidarity'. In this case the self-control by those involved will be relatively high.

This division appears to be a useful one, not only, as here, in comparing and explaining the development of states and markets, but also in examining smaller units such as organizations and families. Research into conflicting company styles by the Organization and Policy Department of the Sociology Institute at the University of Amsterdam showed that the division was useful when comparing Dutch and foreign companies established in the Netherlands. But just as here, a fourth dimension, that of control, also appeared necessary. This was used to express the degree of formality, a particularly important factor when discussing German attitudes. The division is used in this book primarily as an indicator; in order to be used in any other context it would need to be further developed.

Compare for the three-way division Johan Goudsblom, *Sociology in the Balance*, Oxford, 1977, especially Chapter 5.

INDEX

Page references in bold denotes major section/chapter devoted to subject.

agricultural policy 59, **92–127**; breaking of conspiracy of silence over subsidies 109–11, 113; closer scrutiny of subsidy monitoring procedures 113–15; denial of access to data 115; EAGGF report 99–103; early success 57, 98–100; estimated income transfers between EU member states as result of 100t; exchange programme between national customs 113–14; fraud 92–4, 112–13, 126; French influence on 56, 57, 94–5; improvement in subsidy monitoring 111–12; insufficient monitoring of subsidy payments 93, 97–8, 103, 104, 114–15; introduction of 5 per cent physical inspection of exports 114, 120, 123; national differences over monitoring 99, 111–12, **115–25**; payment of subsidies 96–7; reasons for growth in number of reported irregularities 109–11; report on monitoring of subsidized exports 92–4, 113; reported irregularities to EAGGF 100, 101t–2t, 103, 104, 105–8; secrecy over subsidy monitoring 99; slowness of accounting procedures 100; subsidies as binding agent 94–6, 109; subsidy control procedures 125–7; tariffs 55, 60, 64, 95; *see also* individual countries

aristocracy: diminishing of influence 47; possession of hunting weapons 81; status of in England and France 28, 29–30;

arms race 62

asylum policies 89

Belgium: agricultural subsidy monitoring 106, 109, 117, 123; compulsory identification 79; customs service 123; division between Flemings and Walloons 122–3, 139, 180–1n; and European integration 139–40; hunting weapon regulations 81; judicial system 77, 78, 82; public prosecution service 119; reported irregularities to EAGGF 106, 122; and Schengen Treaty negotiations 77, 78–9; weakness of state apparatus 78–9

border controls, abandonment of 171; increased potential of crime due to 71–2, 85; *see also* Schengen, Treaty of

Bretton Woods Agreement (1944) 51, 62

187

Britain 2, **26–32**, 124–5, 165;
agricultural subsidy monitoring
108, 125; aristocracy 28, 29–30;
attitude to European
integration 53, 110–11, 124–5,
140; comparisons with France
in centralization of state 28–30;
'control culture' in dealing with
other countries 31; customs
service 30, 31; development of
egalitarian centralism 26–7,
28–30; and ECCS 52–3; and
EMS 140; expansion of early
free market 17–18, 28–9, 30, 31,
50; on expansion of European
Union 1; judicial apparatus 41,
42, 43; rejection of EC
application by France 60–1, 95;
relationship between trade
liberalisation and nationalism
108, 124; state formation 26,
27–8; and WEU 55
Bundesbank 66, 135, 142
business 154; and European
integration 146–7

Charlemagne 12, 23
Charles I, 30
China 16
civilization, European **158–73**;
ambivalence towards 159, 165,
170; characteristics 158;
collective punishment example
166–7, 168; contrast in
immigration policy 162–3, 164;
contrasts in 169–70;
dependence on United States
171; and downward spiral
scenario 69, 71; effect on
national civilizations 164–6;
exchange of 167–9; fallacy of
cultural norm of equality
161–4; and Freud 161; growth
in certainty 19–20, 159, 163–4,
170; history of concept 159–61;
and hostage model 171–2;
noble savage myth 160–1;
opposing interests 167–9;
relationship between

integration and 18, 20, 158–9,
164–5, 169; relationship with
state 19–20, 21; and violence
169–70; vulnerability of market
without army 171–3
Colbert, Jean-Baptiste 25, 107
Cold War 50, 152, 155
collective punishment 166–7, 168
Comecon 50
Commission, European: and
agricultural subsidy monitoring
97, 100, 112, 113, 114, 119, 122;
role 57; White Book on
economic recovery (1993)
153–4
competition–monopoly
mechanism 91, 155; Eastern
Europe 50; Europe 12–14;
France 22; and state formation
10–12
Council of Ministers 58, 131, 132
Court of Justice 57
crime: consequences of increase
in 72–3; cross-border pursuit
operations 85–6, 87; drug
policies 43, **82–4**; hunting
weapon regulations 81–2, 83,
122; increased potential of due
to abandonment of border
controls 71–2, 85; information
system on criminals 87; judicial
cooperation between countries
over 86–7; and Schengen
Treaty negotiations 75, 85
cross-border pursuit operations
85–6, 87
customs service 113–14;
abandonment of border
controls *see* Schengen, Treaty
of; and agricultural subsidy
monitoring controls 113–14;
formation of 21–2; role of 20;
see also individual countries
customs union *see* Zollverein

Dankert, Piet 110
De Gaulle, President 60
De Swaan, A. 181–2n, 186n
defence: European Defence

Community 53–5, 94
Delors, Jacques 153
Denmark 2, 165; agricultural
  subsidy monitoring 108, 125;
  compared with Netherlands
  133–4; highly developed sense
  of justice 167, 168; joins EC 61;
  referendum on Maastricht
  Treaty 136, 143 relationship
  with Community 123–4, 134;
  reported irregularities to
  EAGGF 108, 123; state
  machinery 133
détente: and European integration
  62
downward spiral scenario 69, 72;
  and agricultural subsidy
  monitoring 98, 99, 104
drug policies 43, 76, **82–4**
Dutch *see* Netherlands

EAGGF report *see* European
  Agricultural Guidance and
  Guarantee Fund report
Eastern Europe 14, 51, 150–1,
  170; disintegration of 148,
  150–1; dominance of Soviet
  Union 50; effect of
  disintegration on European
  integration 151, 153; progress
  in 62, 65; relationship with
  Western Europe 151–3
ECCS (European Community for
  Coal and Steel) 52–3, 55
economic integration 55, 65 *see
  also* EMU
economy: and European
  integration 146–7
EDC (European Defence
  Community) 53–5, 94
education 168
Elias, Norbert 5, 179n, 186n
EMS (European Monetary
  System) 1, 59, 135, 136, 137, 140
EMU (European Monetary
  Union) 135–6, 137
Energy Charter 153
England *see* Britain
esprit de corps 20

Europe: conflicting views over
  vision of 1; history of relations
  between state and market
  16–18; 'political fragmentation'
  16–17; post war initiatives
  towards integration 46–7; state
  formation 12–14; US policy
  towards 48–9
European Agricultural Guarantee
  Fund (EAGGF) report 99–103;
  reported irregularities 100,
  101t–102t, 103
European Central Bank 135
European civilization *see*
  civilization, European
European Commission *see*
  Commission, European
European Community **55–62**, 170;
  agricultural policy 56, 60, 94,
  110; aim of establishing free
  market 3, 46, 55, 59–60;
  discrepancy between negative
  and positive integration 4, 5,
  59–60, 65, 69–70, 91; founding
  46, 55; French influence on
  56–7, 94; increase in prestige of
  170; intergovernmental
  character 3, 55, 57–9, 60;
  majority voting system 58;
  managerial weakness 119;
  relationship with West Germany
  55–6, 57; and Single European
  Act 4, 5, 63–4, 65, 66, 73, 131,
  147, 154; slow progress 61; and
  US 61–2
European Community for Coal
  and Steel (ECCS) 52–3, 55
European Court of Auditors:
  report on monitoring of
  subsidized export of
  agricultural products 92–4, 113,
  114
European Court of Justice 57, 113
European Defence Community
  (EDC) 53–5, 94
European Economic Community
  1–2, 3, 47, 55
European integration *see*
  integration, European

European Monetary System *see* EMS

European Monetary Union *see* EMU

European Parliament 65–6; strengthening of powers 58, 131, 132, 133, 134

European Political Union 133, 134

Federal Republic of Germany *see* West Germany

federalism 1, 55, 61, 132–5

Femac rule 116

First World War 48

fish scandal 118

foreigners, admission of *see* immigration

'Forum Americanum' 52, 61, 63

France 1, **22–6**; accessibility of terrain leads to early vulnerability 27; agricultural policy 56, 57, 94–5; agricultural subsidy monitoring 106–7, 108, 117, 121; authoritarian character of system 42, 121–2; ban on migrant children wearing headscarves to school 163; clash with Dutch federalist view of Europe 61; customs service 26, 31, 106, 121–2; development of free market 17–18, 24, 25–6; differences between Britain concerning centralization 28–30; economic relationships 23; and EDC 53, 54, 94; effect of expansion of European Union on 157; and European Community 56–7, 94; hierarchical centralism 22–3, 24–5, 26, 27, 28, 37, 77; hunting weapon restrictions 81, 83; integration process during Napoleonic era 13; introduction of first general direct taxation 24; judicial apparatus 41–3, 77, 82; link between monetarization and centralization 23–4; mercantilism 24, 25, 107; and

NATO 53; public prosecution service 119; referendum on Maastricht Treaty 136–9, 142, 156; rejection of British application for EC membership 60–1, 95; and Schengen Treaty negotiations 77–8; state formation 22, 27–8; and United States 95; view of European integration 144; visa laws 77–8, 88, 89

Frankish empire 22

French Continental System 26

Freud, Sigmund 160

GATT conference 60

German Central Bank *see* Bundesbank

Germany 1, 18, 33, **37–40**, 65, 94; agricultural subsidy monitoring 105–6, 107, 109, 120–1; anxiety from member states over 141–2; asylum policy 89; cross-border police pursuit operations 85–6; difficulty in early centralization 37–8; early unification 46–7; and European agricultural policy 95, 96, 100, 105; and European integration 142, 144; firearm regulations 81; formation of customs union (Zollverein) 38–9; influence of nobility 38; integration of Community legislation into national legislation 105; judicial apparatus 41–3, 119; move towards legalistic centralism 39–40, 105; origin of authoritarian ethos 42; post war integration process 13; refugee policy 141; reunification 151; and Schengen Treaty negotiations 74–5, 77; state and market formation 37–40; strong involvement in European Union 74–5; and United States 48; visa laws 88–9; *see also* West Germany

Gorbachev, Michail 148, 149

grain: inspection of *Kapitan Danilkin* ship, 92–3
Greece 63, 118
Groningen 34
Gulf War 151

Habsburg, House of 16, 32, 34, 180n
Hamburg 121
Hanseatic League 16
Hitler, Adolf 13
Holland *see* Netherlands
hostage theory 171–2; and agricultural negotiations 125–7; and integration 155, 156; opposing interests of civilization 168–9; and Schengen Treaty negotiations 90–1
hunting weapons: regulations concerning 81–2, 83, 122

identification, compulsory: national differences over 79–81
immigration 88–9, 162–3, 164
industry: and ECCS 52–3
integration, European 131–57,165–6, 173; contrast with Eastern Europe 150; and *détente* 62; dilemma over 2–4, 60, 62, 64, 65–6, 69,169; development of interest in 1–2; differences in outlook based on national identification 144; discrepancy between negative and positive 4, 5, 59–60, 65, 69–70, 91; early form of 12–14; economic threat sets process in motion 1 46; effect of disintegration of Eastern Europe on 65, 151, 153; external conditions 145–53; gaining of momentum in mid-1980s 62–3, 73; and hostage model 155, 156; intergovernmental form of *see* intergovernmental cooperation; political and military influences 148–53; positive outlook 145;

problems 154–5; problems with post war initiatives towards 46–7; relationship between civilization and 18, 20, 158–9, 164, 169; silence by business over 146–7; stagnation of 61; threat of war by Soviet Union as incentive for early 54; and transfer of sovereignty scenario 70, 72; *see also* Maastricht Treaty
intergovernmental cooperation 70, 73, 131, 135, 145, 152, 154–5; and agricultural monitoring policy 111, 125–6; hostage model 90–1, 125–7, 155, 156; and Schengen Treaty 84–5, 90–1
International Monetary Fund (IMF) 51
interstate negotiations *see* intergovernmental cooperation
Ireland: joins EC 61
Italy 18; agricultural subsidy monitoring 106, 109, 111–12; cities as divided political group 33–4; and ECCS 52

Jews 11
judicial apparatus 41–5, 165; cooperation under Schengen Treaty 86–7; differences between France and Germany 41–3; effect of open borders on 71–2, 85; public prosecution service 118–19; *see also* individual countries

Kennedy Round 60
Kohl, Helmut 142

legal systems *see* judicial apparatus
Liberation 71
Lubbers, Ruud 153

Maastricht Treaty 1, 132–45; Denmark's non-ratification of 136, 143; federative option 132–5; French referendum 136–9, 142, 156; objections to

135–6; position of individual countries on **139–44**; principles 69, 132; seen as compromise 135, 136

Magna Carta (1215) 28, 29

Major, John 140

market(s), **14–18**, 19; development of 'free' in Britain 17–18, 28–9, 30, 31, 50; development of 'free' in France 17–18, 24, 25–6; difficulty in establishing within central authority area 37; disadvantages of 'stateless' 94, 127, 131, 146, 154–5; early establishment of after formation of state 9, 22, 14, 64; early relationship with state 15; establishment of 'stateless' 64–5; formation process 9, **14–18**, 20; in Germany 37, 38–9; importance of taxation to support system 14; in Netherlands 35–7; strong ties between state in Europe 16–19; tension between state and 2–4

Marshall Plan 49, 51

mercantilism 218, 4, 25, 31, 50

Middle East: ancient empires of 11

Mitterrand, François 136, 142

Napolean 13

national sovereignty *see* sovereignty

NATO (North Atlantic Treaty Organization) 51–2, 53, 60, 151, 165

negotiations *see* intergovernmental cooperation

Netherlands **32–7**, **115–20**, 122, 124, 165, 180–1n; accusation of unfair competition of Rotterdam 117–18; and agricultural policy of European Community 57, 95; agricultural subsidy monitoring 116–18, 119, 120; asylum policy 89; attitude towards Zollverein 43–4; centralizing of state 37; compared with Denmark 133–4; customs service 37, 119; and developed sense of justice 167–8; difficulty in struggle towards centralization 34; drugs policy 76, 82–4; egalitarian federalism 32, 37, 116; and European Parliament 65–6; favourable attitude towards European integration 141, 143–4, 145; and federalism 61, 132–4; fire-arms regulations 81–2; fish scandal 118; formation of internal market 35–7; and France 61; judicial system 75, 79, 82, 84, 90, 119; and Maastricht Treaty 143; migrant policy 162–3; public prosecution service 119; rejection of compulsory identification 79, 80, 81; reservations over EDC 54–5; and Schengen Treaty negotiations 75–6, 79; state formation 16, 32–3, 34; success of republic movement 32–4; and Union of Utrecht 32, 34, 35; visa policy 89

'noble savage', myth of 160–1

Normandy, Duke of 27

North German Confederation 40

Northern Ireland 108

OECD (Organization for Economic Cooperation and Development) 52

OEEC (Organization for European Economic Cooperation) 52

Old Testament: insight into early state formation 11–12

'open borders' policy 71–2, 171; *see also* Schengen, Treaty of

Organization for Economic Cooperation and Development (OECD) 52

'paradox of collective action', 90, 91

Partnership for Peace programme 151

Philips 63
police force 20, 41; cross-border pursuit operations 85–6, 87; development linked to state 20–1
Portugal 63
Prussia 37–8, 39–40, 41, 47
public prosecution system 118–19

Republic of the United Provinces 32–3 *see also* Netherlands
Roman Empire 12
Rome, Treaty of (1957) 55, 56, 57, 60
Rotterdam 43–4, 116: accusation of unfair competition of 117–18
Rushdie, Salman 163
Russia 152, 153 *see also* Soviet Union

scenarios 69–70
Schengen, Treaty of 73–91, 125, 127; [communal agreements 84–9: controls on external borders 87–8; cross-border pursuit operations 85–6, 87; judicial cooperation 86–7; visa and asylum policies 88–9, 90]; conclusions 90–1; delay in implementation 85, 90; [negotiations 74–9: Belgium 77, 78–9; compulsory identification 79–81; drug policies 82–4; France 77–8; Germany 74–5, 77; hunting weapon regulations 81–2, 83; Netherlands 75–6, 79]; significance of 73
Schengen information system 87
Scotland 26
sea trade 17
Second World War: and European integration 1–2, 46–7
Single European Act (1986) 4, 5, 63–4, 65, 66, 73, 131, 147, 154
Smith, Adam 18, 63, 175n
social welfare facilities 168
sovereignty 58, 66, 150; refusal of transfer 2–3, 4, 85, 98; scenario of transfer 70, 72–3

Soviet Union 51; alliance with Eastern Europe 50; reasons for disintegration 65, 148–9; relationship with US 49–50, 62; threat of war posed by as incentive for integration 54
Spain 1, 34, 63
state formation: based on violence 9–10, 14; competition–monopoly mechanism 10–12; early relationship with market 15; establishment of market after 9, 14, 22, 64; Europe 12–14; Old Testament insights into 11–12; processes of 9–14; strong ties between market and 16–19; tension between market and 2–4; *see also* individual countries
subsidies, agricultural 93, 96–8, 99, 126; breaking of conspiracy of silence over 109–11, 113; closer scrutiny of monitoring procedures 113–15; as Community's binding agent 94–6, 109; conspiracy of silence 99, 109; expenditure 100; insufficient monitoring procedures 93, 97–8, 103, 104, 114–15; national differences over monitoring 99, 111–12, 115–25; payment of 96–7; report on monitoring of subsidized exports 92–4, 113; reported irregularities to EAGGF 100, 101t–2t, 103, 104, 105–8; *see also* individual countries
Switzerland 35

taille 24, 28
tariffs, agricultural 55, 60, 64, 95
taxation 64; and market formation 14, 15, 16, 17
Thatcher, Margaret 110–11, 124, 140

unions: power reduced at European level 147
United nations 152, 162

United States 1, **47–51**, 146, 151–2; conflict over agricultural tariffs 60, 95; dependence on by European states 54, 171; detachment from Treaty of Rome 60; diminishing of dominance 61–2; economic stagnation 109–10; establishment 48; and France 95; and Germany 48; involvement in First World War 48; and Marshall Plan 49, 51; monetary controller of 'global free market' 50–1; and NATO 51–2, 53; post war policy towards European integration 48–9, 51–2, 55, 60, 95; and Soviet Union 49–50, 62; view of EDC 53–4
Utrecht, Union of, 32, 34, 35

Verdun, Treaty of 12

violence: motivation for state formation 9–10, 12, 14
visa laws **88–9**, 90; French 77–8, 88, 89

war: motivation for state formation 9–10, 12, 14
Warsaw pact 50, 51
West Germany: member of NATO 54; role in European Community 55–6, 57; *see also* Germany
Western European Union (WEU) 55
White Book on economic recovery (European Commission) 153–4
World Trade Organization (WTO) 147

Zollhilfspersonal 121
Zollverein (customs union) 38–9, 40, 43, 44, 114, 121